Chicago Sociology

1920–1932

Chandler Publications in
ANTHROPOLOGY AND SOCIOLOGY
Leonard Broom, *Editor*

Chicago Sociology

~(1920–1932)~

■

Robert E. L. Faris

University of Washington

CHANDLER PUBLISHING COMPANY
124 SPEAR STREET, SAN FRANCISCO, CALIFORNIA 94105

CONTENTS

CONTENTS

PORTRAITS

(immediately following the Preface)

Albion W. Small (1854–1926)

William I. Thomas (1863–1947)

George H. Mead (1863–1931)

Robert E. Park (1864–1944)

Ernest W. Burgess (1886–1966)

Ellsworth Faris (1874–1953)

William F. Ogburn (1886–1959)

Louis Wirth (1897–1952)

EDITOR'S FOREWORD

If sociologists are to understand how their discipline has developed, more attention must be given to replacing myth with fact and tradition with written account. As the formative years and men of American sociology disappear from living memory, reconstruction becomes more difficult and tradition becomes stylized and thin. Some may feel that what does not endure in often-cited publications does not warrant their attention, but the Chicago tradition was to a great extent an oral tradition whose crystallization in expository works is still being written by second and third generations of student descendants. Even today sociologists who depend on the *publications* of the Chicago school are instructed that corrective qualifications have long since been made by Robert E. Park and Ernest W. Burgess—in lectures. One should also bear in mind that we are dependent on a posthumous salvage operation for much of our knowledge of the thinking of George Herbert Mead. How much must have escaped the notes of his faithful students in those days before the tape recorder! The secondary transmission of Mead's and Park's and Wirth's ideas from lectures to students' notes to students' books was a long, slow process and it is still going on.

This book is of far more than antiquary interest. It recounts the most important single episode in the past of American sociology. Those who were not in Chicago at that time will gain a sense of what they missed from this straightforward account. Those who were there can test their own memories, add details, and emphasize different lights or shadows.

Perhaps no sociologist is better qualified than Robert Faris to write this book. Luck put him in the right house in the right place at the right time. Talent, inclination, and socialization drew his attention to Chicago sociology and the sociologists in this book. There are few whose lives have been so completely taken up with sociology and with Chicago sociology.

Although living memory lies in the background of Faris's writing and contributes to the value of the book, the reader will not find here gossip or inside information about life on the Midway. William I. Thomas, we are told, left Chicago, and that is all. Struggles between strong personalities are unmentioned. It is only hinted, as some of us outsiders have heard, that students left Park's office shattered from their encounters with that forceful figure. The omission of such details, and of their critical assessment, is intentional. Faris faithfully tells only the part of the story he thinks pertinent to sociology. As T. V. Smith put it, "Gossip might be said to be the mother of social science; for gossip is the easy way to celebrate changes already transpired and to make two events grow where but one grew before. [But] . . . social science may . . . be distinguished from gossip in terms of exactitude and disinterestedness." The mood of this book is in the tradition of social science rather than of gossip.

Some questions that may be consequential are judged by the author to be outside his task. The matter of the interrelations of Chicago sociology and Midwest neo-realism is not developed. It is tempting to consider the possible consequences of the past dominance of the discipline by a single department. How far has the present sociological predicament been conditioned by the Chicago self-confidence of an earlier period and the loyalties for (and against) the department? Has a posture of defensiveness against any apparent concentration of power persisted in part because most of the resources were once in one place to be used or abused with little external constraint? The answers are not obvious. The Chicago department was certainly the best thing in American sociology for a long time, but it is less than certain that it was therefore an unalloyed benefit for the advancement of the discipline. Although Faris does not deal with the question, the appearance of the book may invite a timely reconsideration of the sources of dissensus in American sociology and from a longer time perspective.

The book communicates the sense of the Chicago department as a going concern. Graduate education at Chicago was a research experience under the most personal kind of pedagogy. The students played their part in a continuing research enterprise, got their hands dirty with data, and learned to cope under demanding task masters. The lists of graduates remind us that it was the seedbed of American sociology. In 1920 the department consisted of just three men (but what men!)—Park, Burgess, and Ellsworth Faris—who that year turned out five Doctors of Philosophy and three Masters of Arts. Perusal of the appended lists of 113 Doctors of Philosophy and 202 Masters of Arts from the beginning to 1935 evokes nostalgia, delight, and wonder. W. I. Thomas received his degree in 1896 with a dissertation entitled *On a Difference of the Metabolism of the Sexes.* In 1901 Charles Joseph Bushnell wrote *A Study of the Stock Yards Community at Chicago, as a Typical Example of the Bearing of Modern Industry upon Democracy, with Constructive Suggestions.* There were vintage years: 1913, with E. W. Burgess, J. F. Steiner, and E. H. Sutherland; 1928, with eight Doctors of Philosophy, including Robert Redfield, J. H. Mueller, Everett Hughes, and Herbert Blumer. With these lists the reader can play his own games: "Where Is He Now?" "*That* Was Sociology?" "Were They Writing about THAT *Then?*" and, regretfully, "Why Didn't He Ever Write Anything Else?" It might be provident for the Chicago library to duplicate the microfilms of its old theses in anticipation of a sharp increase in requests from borrowers.

This book is the account of the most successful kind of personal pedagogy, of the development of standards in a nascent discipline, and of a department that became a social movement. In Chicago, sociology was implanted in American academic life and after that nothing was quite the same again.

LEONARD BROOM

PREFACE

The purpose of this volume is to describe the way in which the Department of Sociology at the University of Chicago came into its dominant position in American sociology and to attempt a partial explanation of this renaissance at Chicago. The author seeks to be objective and does not intend to provide appreciation for or tribute to worthy men or to an organization, but only to describe what happened and how.

The attempt to explain the accomplishment of the transition from a pre-scientific to a scientific stage in sociology may properly be conceived of as a modest step in the sociology of science. Some useful lessons may be learned from an examination of both the similarities and differences in the courses of unlike sciences. The comparisons will not be made here, but the material is written with the possibility of such comparisons in mind. It is assumed that it is desirable that sociologists, along with all other scientists, understand what they are doing and how it relates to other activities of men.

The period of interest has no precise beginning or end, but the temporal focus of the inquiry is on the few years in which the Chicago department achieved a strong research momentum and held a sort of temporary performance championship in the United States, which in that time also meant the world leadership of sociology. The period of interest therefore extends approximately from the early 1920's until some time in the middle 1930's. There is no decline and fall of the Chicago department in the latter part of this era, but rather a healthy emergence of excellence and productivity in sociology departments at other strong universities. Some of these departments evolved their own special characteristics and took the leadership in certain aspects of sociology, but none were unaffected by the earlier accomplishments at Chicago. There is history to be written elsewhere, of course, but the immediate task centers on Chicago.

The author was a student at Chicago during the heart of this period —as undergraduate from 1924–1928 and graduate student from 1928–1931. He encountered a few lectures on sociology in his first undergraduate year in a general science course and took the introductory sociology course from the late Eyler N. Simpson in his second year. In completing an undergraduate major as well as a doctorate, he was exposed to nearly all of the courses taught in the department and was influenced by every member of the departmental faculty as well as some visiting professors from other universities, among them R. D. McKenzie, the vigorous developer of ecological theory, and Maurice Halbwachs, the leading successor to Émile Durkheim and professor at the University of Paris. Personal experiences necessarily contribute to this work and inevitably must color the interpretation despite all resolution to preserve objectivity.

The study was undertaken at the suggestion of Leonard Broom, who contributed valuable suggestions and technical improvements in the manuscript, for which the author is grateful. Acknowledgment is also due to the following former Chicago students who contributed from their memories to the project: Stuart A. Queen, Jacob F. Balzer, Herbert Blumer, Everett C. Hughes, Helen MacGill Hughes, Philip M. Hauser, Carroll D. Clark, Norman S. Hayner, Andrew W. Lind, Katherine Niles Lind, Margaret Park Redfield, Jan E. Dizard, and Ernest W. Burgess. Portraits were supplied through the courtesy of Alice Myers of the American Sociological Association office, Eleanor Isbell of the Social Science Research Council, and Ann Colley of the University of Chicago Library. For aid in the extensive correspondence and in the preparation of the manuscript the author is indebted to Gwen A. Williams and to Beulah E. Reddaway. Finally, the list of acknowledgments would be incomplete without an admission that over thirty years of conversations with Ellsworth Faris before his death in 1953 provide an important proportion of background material.

ROBERT E. L. FARIS

University of Washington

SOME LEADING
PERSONALITIES OF
CHICAGO SOCIOLOGY

Albion Woodbury Small
1854–1926

ALBION WOODBURY SMALL was born in Buckfield, Maine, son of A. K. P. Small and Thankful Lincoln (Woodbury). He trained for the ministry at Colby College and graduated in 1876. Then he studied history in Berlin and Leipzig from 1879 until he returned to the United States in 1881 to study at Johns Hopkins. In 1887 he married Valerie von Massow, daughter of a German general. He completed his Ph.D. in history at Johns Hopkins in 1889 and served as president and professor of history at Colby College from 1889 to 1892. At Colby he became interested in sociology and chose to teach it. At this time he published a handbook titled *An Introduction to the Science of Sociology*—the same title used three decades later by Park and Burgess.

In 1890 Small was interviewed by William Rainey Harper concerning the possibility of an appointment to the faculty of the new University of Chicago. Small persuaded Harper that the University should introduce sociology into the curriculum, and thus he was invited to become head professor of sociology, starting with the opening of the University in 1892. He was also named dean, and soon afterward, dean of the graduate school. He served in this appointment until his retirement in 1925. During his career he founded the *American Journal of Sociology*, edited this publication from 1895 to 1925, and served as president of the American Sociological Society for two terms in 1912 and 1913. His principal books were *General Sociology*, 1905, and *Origins of Sociology*, 1924. Small was considered especially influential in bringing German sociology to the attention of American scholars, but his largest contribution may have been in building the leading department of sociology.

University of Chicago Library Photo,
Ann Colley

William Isaac Thomas

1863–1947

WILLIAM ISAAC THOMAS was born on a farm in Russell County, Virginia, son of Thaddeus Peter Thomas and Sarah (Price). He was educated at the University of Tennessee, graduating in 1884. From 1888 to 1889 he undertook graduate study at Berlin and Göttingen. He returned to the United States to teach English at Oberlin College from 1889 to 1893 and then went to the University of Chicago to complete his graduate education, receiving a doctorate in 1896. In 1895 he was an instructor in sociology at Chicago and by 1910 he was a professor. Early in the twentieth century he began his studies of assimilation and, in collaboration with Florian Znaniecki, gathered materials on Polish peasants and immigrants to the United States.

In 1918 he left the University of Chicago and undertook research in New York City on Americanization. In 1923 he lectured at the New School for Social Research and later did occasional teaching at Columbia and Harvard Universities. In 1927 he served as president of the American Sociological Society. He retired to Berkeley, California, in 1942.

Thomas's principal works were *Source Book for Social Origins*, 1909; *The Polish Peasant in Europe and America* (with F. Znaniecki), 1918; *The Unadjusted Girl*, 1923; and *Primitive Behavior*, 1937.

Thomas's example in the massive gathering of data played an important part in turning the sociological tradition away from the speculative building of systems. He was also notably influential through his introduction of such useful concepts as *social disorganization, definition of the situation,* and *life-organization,* and through his formulation of the four fundamental wishes, which were popular during the 1920's.

*Social Science Research Council Photo,
Eleanor Isbell*

George Herbert Mead

1863–1931

GEORGE HERBERT MEAD was born in South Hadley, Massachusetts, son of Hiram Mead and Elizabeth Storrs (Billings). He had a classical education at Oberlin, where his father was a professor of homiletics, and graduated in 1883. He taught school briefly and then for a time did surveying and tutoring in the northwest. In 1887 he entered Harvard for additional study with William James and Josiah Royce and graduated the following year. During his extensive travels abroad, he included some study of philosophy, although he did not obtain a doctorate. In 1891 he became an instructor in philosophy at the University of Michigan; then in 1894 he joined the faculty at Chicago at the invitation of John Dewey and spent the rest of his career there until his death in 1931.

Mead wrote little, and, except for a few papers generally overlooked by sociologists, his life contribution is recorded in three books compiled by students and colleagues after his death. His influence on sociology was almost entirely from the content of his course on Advanced Social Psychology, which was attended by most Chicago graduate students in sociology. In this course, repeated annually for at least a quarter of a century, he presented his evolving thoughts which constitute the book *Mind, Self, and Society,* published by the University of Chicago Press in 1934. Drawing from his friends John Dewey and Charles Horton Cooley, Mead gave a valuable formulation to the problem of how the human mind and self may be said to arise in a process of social interaction. His contribution was supported and elaborated by Ellsworth Faris and by Herbert Blumer, both former students in Mead's famous course, and later by their students.

Robert Ezra Park ═══════════════

1864–1944

ROBERT EZRA PARK was born in Luzerne County, Pennsylvania, son of Hiram Asa Park and Theodosia (Warner). After graduating from the University of Michigan in 1887 he worked for a time as newspaper reporter. In 1894 he married Clara Cahill. He soon resumed study and earned an M.A. at Harvard in 1899. After a period at Heidelberg he achieved a Ph.D. in 1904 and spent the next year as an assistant in philosophy at Harvard University. From 1905 to 1914 he served as secretary and companion to Booker T. Washington; then from 1914 until his retirement in 1933 he taught sociology at the University of Chicago. In 1925 he was president of the American Sociological Society. After his retirement Park traveled and taught intermittently as a visiting professor at Fisk University.

Park's principal published works were his doctoral dissertation, *Masse und Publikum*, 1904; *Introduction to the Science of Sociology* (with E. W. Burgess), 1921; and many influential papers on crowd behavior, human ecology, race relations, the newspaper, and other topics. Of particular importance is the paper "The City: Suggestions for the Investigation of Human Behavior in the Urban Environment," published in the *American Journal of Sociology* in 1915. This paper furnished important encouragement to the surge of urban research at Chicago during the following two decades. Park's papers were published in three posthumous volumes, *Race and Culture*, 1950; *Human Communities*, 1952; and *Society*, 1955 (all published by the Free Press of Glencoe, Illinois). An even larger part of Park's contribution to scholarly production was made through his influence on many able students.

University of Chicago Library Photo, Ann Colley

Ernest Watson Burgess

1886–1966

ERNEST WATSON BURGESS was born in Tilbury, Ontario, son of Edmund James Burgess and Mary Ann Jane (Wilson). He graduated from King-fisher College in 1908 and undertook graduate study at the University of Chicago, completing the Ph.D. in 1913. He taught at Toledo University, 1912–1913; University of Kansas, 1913–1915; and at Ohio State University, 1915–1916. In 1919 he joined the faculty of the University of Chicago, where he remained until his retirement in 1957.

Burgess served as president of the American Sociological Society in 1934 and of the Sociological Research Association in 1942. In 1945–1946 he was chairman of the Social Science Research Council.

His principal published works were *Introduction to the Science of Sociology* (with R. E. Park), 1921; *The City* (with R. E. Park), 1925; *Predicting Success or Failure in Marriage* (with L. S. Cottrell, Jr.), 1939; and *The Family* (with H. J. Locke), 1945. During much of his career at Chicago, Burgess shared an office with Park and collaborated on many sociological activities besides their noted textbook. He played an important part in stimulating the urban studies and also was responsible for the promotion of much research in the field of the family and social disorganization. In his later years on the faculty and after retirement, he participated in important research activity on aging and retirement and related matters. As in the case of Park, much of his contribution was made through his able and productive students.

Ellsworth Faris

1874–1953

ELLSWORTH FARIS was born in Salem County, Tennessee, son of George Alexander Faris and Sophie (Yarborough). The family moved to Texas in 1886, where Faris attended Add-Ran University (later named Texas Christian University) and graduated in 1894. He had intended to become a civil engineer, but under the influence of a visiting evangelist he made a sudden decision to become a missionary and was sent to the Belgian Congo where he served at a station at Coquilhatville. While home on furlough in 1901, he married Elizabeth Homan, who returned with him to the Congo. Following his missionary career, Faris taught philosophy at Texas Christian University from 1904 to 1911. Then he undertook graduate study in philosophy and psychology at the University of Chicago, completing the Ph.D. in psychology in 1914 under John Dewey, George H. Mead, James R. Angell, and others. He taught in the department of psychology at the State University of Iowa, 1914–1915; at Chicago, 1915–1916; and again at Iowa, 1916–1919.

On the resignation of W. I. Thomas from Chicago, Faris was invited to become a sociologist at Chicago to maintain the tradition of social psychology. In 1925 he became chairman of the department, and in 1926 he became editor of the *American Journal of Sociology*. In 1937 he served as president of the American Sociological Society. Although in all his career he never completed a book, he contributed several strongly influential articles, including "The Nature of Human Nature," "Are Instincts Data or Hypotheses?" "The Sect and the Sectarian," and "Of Psychological Elements."

William Fielding Ogburn

1886–1959

WILLIAM FIELDING OGBURN was born in Butler, Georgia, son of Charlton G. Ogburn and Irene Florence (Wynn). He graduated from Mercer University in 1905. In 1910 he married Rubyn Reynolds. His graduate studies at Columbia under Giddings ended when he completed his doctorate in 1912. From 1910 to 1912 he taught economics, politics, and history at Princeton University. Thereafter he held positions at Reed College, 1912–1917; at the University of Washington, 1917–1918; and with the Federal Government in Washington, D.C., 1918–1919. He was a professor of Sociology at Columbia University from 1919 to 1927 and at the University of Chicago from 1927 until his retirement in 1951. He served as chairman of the department from 1936 to 1951. After retirement he traveled extensively and held teaching positions at Oxford University, the University of Calcutta, the University of Delhi, and Florida State University.

Ogburn was president of the American Sociological Society in 1929 and of the American Statistical Association in 1931. He served as chairman of the Social Science Research Council, 1937–1939. From 1930 to 1933 he was director of research of the President's Research Committee on Social Trends and editor of the resulting volume, *Recent Social Trends in the United States,* published in 1933. Other principal works were *Social Change,* 1922; *Sociology* (with M. F. Nimkoff), 1940; *American Society in Wartime* (ed.), 1943; and *Technology and International Relations,* 1949. In his teaching Ogburn was noted for his emphasis on statistics and scientific methods, and he was influential in spreading the scientific spirit in academic sociology at Chicago.

Louis Wirth

1897–1952

LOUIS WIRTH was born in Gemünden, Germany, son of Joseph Wirth and Rosalie (Lorig). In 1911 he came to the United States to join relatives in Omaha, Nebraska. He entered the University of Chicago in 1914, studying sociology with Park, Burgess, Thomas, and Small, and social psychology with Mead. After graduation he was employed for a time in the Bureau of Personal Services of the Jewish Charities of Chicago, serving as director of the division for delinquent boys.

In 1923 Wirth married Mary Bolton of Paducah, Kentucky. He returned to the University of Chicago and completed his doctorate in sociology in 1925. In this period he taught part time at the University and also at the downtown YMCA College. In 1926 he was appointed assistant professor at the University of Chicago. He taught at Tulane University from 1928 to 1930 and spent 1930–1931 in France and Germany on a Social Science Research Council fellowship. He returned to Chicago as an associate professor of Sociology and spent the rest of his career there. He served as president of the American Sociological Society in 1946 and became the first president of the International Sociological Association in 1950.

His principal works were *The Ghetto*, 1928; *Ideology and Utopia* (with K. Mannheim), 1936; and many articles on urbanism, race relations, international relations, and the history of sociological thought.

University of Chicago Library Photo, Ann Colley

Chicago Sociology

1920–1932

American Sociology at the Turn of the Century

In the nineteenth century the academic writings on sociological matters appeared mainly under the name of moral philosophy until Auguste Comte devised the term sociology, thereby in effect committing scholars to create such a specific science. Herbert Spencer, Henry Maine, Gabriel Tarde, Émile Durkheim, Georg Simmel, and other thinkers overseas diligently took up the task, and while they cannot be said to have worked out a completely successful definition of the character of sociology, they convinced the world of scholarship that it was a work that must and could be done. As Albion Small described it, sociology then was "more of a yearning than a substantial body of knowledge, a fixed point of view, or a rigorous method of research." [1] It was an ambitious, vigorous, and confident sort of yearning and for all of its confusion of direction, this groping phase may have been a necessary stage. The discovery of right paths may be helped by making tentative explorations of the wrong roads.

In the later years of the nineteenth century, American scholars joined in the work of creating sociology. Among the most prominent of

[1] Albion W. Small, "Fifty Years of Sociology in the United States—1865–1915," *American Journal of Sociology*, May 1916. Reprinted in Index to Volumes I–LII, p. 229.

these men were Lester F. Ward, William Graham Sumner, Franklin H. Giddings, and Edward A. Ross. Each of these scholars was a powerful personality, full of energy and self-confidence, and each was undoubtedly willing to take the leadership in sociology. They all saw the assignment as large and conceived that they needed to give definition to the field, to systematize it and point out the major applications to human welfare and the survival of the always imperiled civilization. All of this work required seven-league boots, and none of these men hestitated to draw them on, leaden though they turned out to be.

These American pioneers had a strong disposition to discover, mainly by reflection, one or a few fundamental and simple principles that would serve as explanation of all human behavior. Ward, for example, asserted as *the* fundamental law of human nature that "all men will, under all circumstances, seek their greatest gain." [2] This law, of course, can stand up only if all human actions, whatever their nature, are artifically provided with an interpretation of gain maximizing. Ward did this by listing as motive forces not only the *essential forces* of desire for food and sex, but also the *nonessential* such as esthetic, moral, and intellectual desires. These categories were broad enough to allow the above argument to be applied, but they were so inclusive as to render the whole attempt in effect circular and therefore useless.

Giddings, in similar spirit, sought to found sociology on the motivating principle he called *consciousness of kind*.[3] Sure of the truth-finding power of his mind he wrote, "the sociological postulate can be no other than this, namely: The original and elementary subjective fact in society is *consciousness of kind*. By this I mean a state of consciousness in which any being, whether low or high in the scale of life, recognizes another conscious being as of like kind with itself." According to Giddings, this principle converts mere gregariousness into society.

Such an argument was carried by Giddings well into the twentieth century, long after Durkheim had shown in his work on the division of

---

[2] Lester F. Ward, *Dynamic Sociology* (New York: D. Appleton and Co., 1897), p. 20.

[3] Franklin H. Giddings, *Principles of Sociology*, (New York: Macmillan, 1896), p. 17.

labor how much of cooperative life among human beings is based on the organization of *complementary differences*.

The nineteenth-century confidence in the power of such armchair speculation is well shown in Giddings's own illustration of the link between perceived similarity and concerted action.[4] [Strangers in the Louvre observing a piece of sculpture by Rodin] "know themselves to be, in appreciation of this beautiful thing, of one kind. A psychological group has been formed by pluralistic reaction to a common stimulation, by interstimulation and responses thereto, and by awareness of a kinship of minds, manifested in similarity of behavior. The psychological group arising in mere like-response, may collectively begin to do something. . . . A purpose to do may be talked over and become concerted volition. Agreeing decision may become concerted action; which may be repeated, and become a folkway." It is somewhat difficult to believe, in view of the final sentence, that Giddings ever actually saw assorted strangers viewing a work of art.

E. A. Ross drew his major inspiration from Tarde, who reasoned that all social life is a matter of *invention* and *imitation* and from the cyclic interplay of these two factors *all of the variety and complexity of social life* comes into being. Tarde felt that this formulation contained "the key to almost every lock" in the social mystery. Ross also failed to see the importance of organization based on complementary differences, and he set out to build his whole sociology on Tarde's doctrine of imitation, the force which seemed to tame the human instincts so that men could cooperate.

Accompanying the search for such basic principles was a hunger for a grand unity of knowledge that would be both esthetically satisfying and generally applicable in solving the major problems of humanity. Most of the nineteenth-century American sociological pioneers competed with Herbert Spencer in this respect. Spencer found his unity and panacea in the concept of evolution—everything is involved in the grand process of evolution, and all we have to do in quest of human welfare is leave it alone. W. G. Sumner is also famous for advocating many kinds of noninterference, although on somewhat different grounds. Ward, however, who was as cosmic in his systematic view as

[4] *Studies in the Theory of Human Society,* (New York: Macmillan, 1922), pp. 158–159.

was Spencer, argued that man could take charge of evolution from his time onward. Ross, Ward's strong admirer and relative by marriage, was also an enthusiastic humanitarian and reformer. In fact it was Ross's crusading tendency that brought him out of economics and into sociology: he wrote Ward in 1897 that the president of Stanford University "took occasion after the horror excited in the East by my free silver advocacy to remove me as far as possible from all connection with Finance by making me Prof. of Sociology." [5]

It is not hard to sense the feverish excitement of these men who thought they were creating such inclusive and valuable systems of thought in the face of attacks by ignorant but powerful rivals. Slow, calm, objective research could hardly be expected in such circumstances. When Ross described to Ward his investigations in Social Control he made no mention of inductive study, but wrote "I am anxious to prove my theses with such a wealth of authorities and evidence that there will be no chance for someone else to write upon it and thrust my exposition of the ideas to one side." [6] Ross gained a large following, produced books, and took part in the education of many students, but he and his contemporaries did not see fully the necessity of having brains speak louder than glands and so they did not play an important part in converting the philosophical subject of sociology into an objective science. This change was to be made later, and an important part of it occurred at Chicago.

These American pioneers did not work in vain, however. They called the attention of the world of scholarship to sociology and in time forced it into the curricula of leading universities. They played a necessary part in wrenching the concern with human behavior from the purely theological viewpoint in which free will and personal responsibility are necessarily unanalyzable to the theory that behavior and society are part of the processes of causation and therefore an explanation is possible. This first work done, other men could more readily take the next steps.

A few nineteenth-century American sociologists were disposed to follow the lead of a line of English writers, philanthropists, and

[5] Bernhard J. Stern, "The Ward-Ross Correspondence II." *American Sociological Review*, XI (October, 1946), 594.
[6] *Ibid.*, 595.

reformers—John Howard, Charles Booth, Beatrice Webb, and others —in exposing evil conditions of society, intervening and helping where they could, and advocating legislative reforms. Religious motives drew some prospective sociologists in this direction. Moreover, the early body of sociologists in the United States recruited numerous restless and dissatisfied clergymen. The combination may account for the considerable pull of early sociology in the humanitarian direction and may also account for the not uncommon linking into one university department of sociology and professional training for social work.

Most of the published work of this humanitarian category was hopelessly emotional. It could, and sometimes did, lead to political action but not toward science; rather, it tended to draw the participants away from science. Booth's description of a London street is characteristic: "An awful place; the worst street in the district. The inhabitants are mostly of lowest class and seem to lack all ideas of cleanliness or decency . . . the children are rarely brought up to any kind of work, but loaf about, and no doubt form the nucleus for future generations of thieves and other bad characters . . . The property is in very bad condition, unsanitary and overcrowded. . . . A number of the rooms are occupied by prostitutes of the most pronounced order." [7] Such an observation tells more about the observer than about the subject of his study.

Research of the Booth type made its contribution toward organizational reform efforts, partly through Fabian Socialism. Apparently it also inspired a grand survey movement in the United States—a development which took its own course, diverging early from academic sociology and finding a close partnership with organized welfare activity.

The Pittsburgh Survey, a massive effort carried out from 1909 to 1914, initiated the movement in the United States. It filled six volumes with information about urban conditions in which there were undesirable features. The topics covered included housing, sanitation, crime and criminal justice, poverty, recreation, wages, industrial accidents, public education, and others. All of this information was gathered in

[7] Charles Booth, *Life and Labour of the People of London*, Volume I (1892), pp. 10–11. Quoted in Pauline V. Young, *Scientific Social Surveys and Research* (New York: Prentice-Hall, 1939), p. 13.

the general spirit of indicating how far below the level of what *ought to be* the existing conditions were and of suggesting ways of improvement through welfare activity and political change.

The Russell Sage Foundation took a strong early interest in this technique and formed a department for making surveys with a full-time director, Shelby M. Harrison. Harrison then quickly undertook a survey of Springfield, Illinois, following a pattern similar to that applied to Pittsburgh but also obtaining wide participation of persons and organizations in the city. With this start the survey pattern gained vogue, and by 1928 Harrison was able to publish a list of 154 general surveys and 2,621 surveys in special fields, such as crime, health, and recreation, carried out in the United States.

Sociologists were aware of the survey movement, but they left most of the activity to welfare workers, administrators, and others. The surveys of cities, however, helped to call the attention of sociologists to the rich materials for investigation, and thus indirectly played a part in preparing the way for the development of urban sociology.

Nineteenth-century sociological thinking might fairly be characterized as speculation about the social implications of variations among individuals. A partial transformation toward true sociology, a halfway step which might be called *collective individualism,* appears in the Tarde-Ross treatment of imitation and in the attraction of the like-minded as seen by Giddings. But these men apparently did not perceive the essential character of organization or its significance as a cause of human behavior. In the case of Ross, this attitude may have been in part the consequence of a sort of doctrinaire blindness, since he was acquainted so well with that part of the French sociological tradition led by Tarde. The intense rivalry between Tarde and Durkheim brought about a factional division in French sociology which hindered the learning of one side from the other, and thus may have influenced Ross to neglect Durkheim.

It was Durkheim, as previously stated, who formulated so clearly the nature of the bond of social cohesion produced by the division of function as well as the one resulting from the attraction of similarities. Persons are drawn together into organizations, not by imitation or like-mindedness, but by the fact that their very differences fit into a complementary pattern in which properties not present in the individuals appear. If any single thought could be said to be at the heart of modern sociology, this would be it. But although Durkheim's book on division of labor appeared in 1893, the Ross-Giddings type of sociologist ignored his basic thought for thirty years and more.

About the turn of the century Charles Horton Cooley set out to give clear formulation to the essence of sociological cohesion in his two books *Human Nature and the Social Order,* published in 1902, and *Social Organization,* published in 1909. In words which still read well today he characterized the nature of primary groups, which are founded on likenesses among members, and of social organizations, which are not. Thus the essential definition of the subject matter of sociology was effectively imported from France by the quiet and modest scholar at the University of Michigan.

At this point it might seem that Michigan should have achieved a considerable lead over other American universities in the building of a sound sociological tradition since in the first decade of the century Cooley appeared to have the clearest vision of its proper direction. But, as is discussed later, a variety of factors play a part in the process, and the diffident and literary Cooley, who was no organizer or promoter, did not offer a model of research activity which graduate students could emulate. His contribution was to the wider world of sociology more than to the Michigan campus.

The foregoing pages summarize the state of United States sociology in the period of infancy of the Chicago department. It was from such a background that the Chicago department founders had to build. Of course they were not able to see this fact as simply or as clearly as we can nearly three-quarters of a century later. When the Chicago department was founded in 1892, the voices of Ward, Sumner, Spencer, and Giddings were still dominant; Durkheim was just one of the sociological voices abroad. None of the original faculty of the Chicago department was trained in sociology because there had been no department to train them. Thus there was still a large amount of uncertainty about what the task was to be—what sort of sociology was to be created. It was to be nearly thirty years more before their successors could feel confident that they were at last on the true road.

The controversy over what sociology should become was also reflected in the variety of men in the original Chicago departmental faculty. They did have in common, however, an optimistic and melioristic attitude toward the modern world. There was theological influence in Albion W. Small and George E. Vincent. Charles R. Henderson had been a minister. Ernest W. Burgess was the son of a minister, as was Ellsworth Faris, who for a time was missionary and minister. Theological concerns show clearly in the titles of some of the early theses, among which are the following three M.A. theses:

Stages in the Theological Development of Martin Luther (1893), Clifford W. Barnes.

The First Three Years of Paul's Career as a Christian (1908), Ruby Lee Lamb.

The Relation of Religion to the "On-Going" of the Social Process (1912), Victor W. Bruder.

Two Ph.D. theses of the period also may have similar inspiration:

The Influence of Modern Social Relations upon Ethical Concepts (1908), Cecil C. North.

Social Policy of Chicago Churches (1911), Samuel N. Reep.

An even larger proportion of theses reflects a humanitarian or welfare concern coming in part from a theological tradition. Among the early M.A. theses of this type may be listed:

Attempt of Chicago to Meet the Positive Needs of the Community (1894), David C. Atkinson.

Factory Legislation for Women in the United States (1897), Annie M. MacLean.

Laboratory Methods in House Sanitation, Together with an Outline of Class-Room Instruction (1898), Henrietta I. Goodrich.

Some Phases of the Sweating System in Chicago (1900), Nellie M. Auten.

The Garbage Problem in Chicago (1902), Fred G. Frink.

Persistence of Poverty (1907), Yetta Scheftel.

Child-Labor in the Cotton Mills of Alabama (1908), Bennett T. Waites.

Doctoral dissertations of similar interest include:

The Social Aim of Education (1898), Ira W. Howerth.

The Social Ideals of Alfred Tennyson as Related to His Time (1899), William C. Gordon.

A Study of the Stock Yards Community at Chicago, as a Typical

Example of the Bearing of Modern Industry upon Democracy, with Constructive Suggestions (1901), Charles J. Bushnell.
Cooperative Credit Associations in the Province of Quebec (1910), Hector MacPherson.
The Relation of Fatigue to Industrial Accidents (1911), Emory S. Bogardus.

The department of sociology had its beginning in the new University of Chicago in 1892. President Harper persuaded a number of outstanding scholars to join his new faculty, one of whom was Albion W. Small, president of Colby College in Maine. When he came to the Chicago campus as Head Professor of Sociology he thereby founded the first department of sociology, undoubtedly stimulating other progressive universities to add this subject in the years immediately following. Sociology took root at Columbia, Kansas, and Michigan within a year or two after the founding at Chicago, and before long also at Yale, Brown, and elsewhere (but not until decades later at Harvard, Princeton, Johns Hopkins, and California). Spencer was writing actively in England, and Ross at Stanford was bringing sociology into his teachings. John Dewey and George H. Mead were teaching at Chicago, making their original contributions to social psychology which were to be of considerable importance to the development of sociology.

Of the sociological leaders of the time in the United States—Ward, Sumner, Giddings, Ross, and Small—the last was perhaps also the least important in making enduring substantive contributions to the field of sociology. Small, born in 1854 in Maryland, had taken a doctorate in history at Johns Hopkins in 1889. A productive scholar, he was especially learned in German philosophy of history and German sociological writings. He usefully imported German literature and wrote on the origins of sociological thinking but failed to convince his colleagues and successors that he had found the real sources of the sociological tradition. With characteristic historian's breadth he wanted to see all social science unified, or at least capable of being so. He was fond, among other things, of referring to the "ongoing of the social process" and paid attention to the processes of conflict and cooperation. He introduced a classification of human motives in his six interests, listing "health, wealth, sociability, knowledge, beauty, and rightness."

Except for the students in Small's classes, however, little or none of this content was found useful by other sociologists, and after his retirement Small's writings were read only by the few persons interested in tracing the development of sociology.

Nevertheless, Small's sociological achievement may well be the greatest among all of his generation of sociological pioneers. The others had the wide audiences, but their writings, too, became obsolescent and it was Small who built the organization that did most to produce modern sociology—more than all of the other traditions combined. In a new university the status order of departments is not as well established as it tends to be in others that are older, and thus Small did not have to begin his work against the disdain and opposition of colleagues in neighboring departments. Sociology at Chicago was completely respectable at the start, as it hardly could have been at Yale, Columbia, Brown, and other universities in which the palpable scorn of the faculty tended to divert able students away from the new and unestablished field of study. But as a former college president, a scholar of repute, and a man of standing on the campus—dean of the graduate school at Chicago and the founder of the *American Journal of Sociology*—Small well deserved the respect of his colleagues.

Students in Small's classes report that he encouraged active research in preference to armchair theorizing and that he proposed to the department that the city of Chicago be used as a major object of research—a thought that was to bear fruit in the 1920's when Park and Burgess were able to give full attention to this aim.

Perhaps equally important in the memory of his students was Small's emphasis on objectivity. He referred to the whole course of sociology since Comte as a "drive toward objectivity" and a proper direction for a developing science. By contrast, Ross, Ward, and Sumner appeared to have little interest in objectivity, and it is hard to imagine any of these three directing their graduate students, as Small is remembered to have done, to proceed as quickly as possible to make everything he taught them out of date.

Small was joined at the start by Charles Richmond Henderson, who was appointed by President Harper without consulting Small. A former minister whose interests were mainly in applied humanitarianism, Henderson left little lasting mark on the history of sociology. He was the only member of the early faculty of the department never to be elected president of the American Sociological Society. He did, however, send students into direct investigations in the various areas of the city, and in this way did his part toward building the habit of active research. Some of the humanitarian interests later shown by Charles Ellwood, Emory Bogardus, and E. W. Burgess may have in part resulted from their study with Henderson. This line of activity, however, has not remained congenial to objective sociology. Academic training in social work, once generally allied with sociology in one department, has almost universally withdrawn into separate departments and schools, leaving behind the chill that is characteristic of the feelings between divorced couples.

A third member of the original department was George E. Vincent, son of the founder of Chautauqua. Like his father, he was an enthusiast for general education and the grand unity of knowledge and a man of great eloquence. Long after his retirement he addressed a sociological convention in a fervent plea that sociologists not lose the sense of unity of knowledge, but the necessity of ever increasing specialization that follows from the increase of information inevitably defeated this ideal. Vincent's influence steadily waned and vanished after his appointment as president of the University of Minnesota in 1911.

The fourth and youngest member of the department was William I. Thomas. Like Vincent, he taught in the department while working on his doctorate and received that degree in 1896. After graduation he remained in the department until 1919 and became its most creative and influential member during that period. He continued to be active and productive for the rest of his life, which ended in 1947 in his eighty-fifth year. He was a powerful, vigorous, inventive, and productive man and, because he was untrammeled by self-criticism, perfectionism, or any of the characteristic inhibitions of conventional academicians, he made a much greater substantive contribution to American sociology than did any of his early colleagues at Chicago. Much material regarding Thomas is available in a series of four articles by Kimball Young, "Contributions of William Isaac Thomas to Sociology," in *Sociology and Social Research*, Vol. 47, No. 4 (October, 1962; January, April, and July, 1963).

Thomas began to develop an interest in sociology while he was teaching English at Oberlin College, and he undertook to study the subject at Chicago with the opening of the university in 1892, taking courses from Small and Henderson. He acquired an early interest in folk-sociology or ethnology, in social psychology, and in the sociology of race and the process of assimilation—these subjects being considerably narrower than the historical sweep of Small and the wide generalizing of Vincent. In his preference for clear-cut and definite principles and findings, Thomas soon developed a strong tendency to make observations on the individual and the variables which influence his actions, and exhibited a preference for biological explanations of individual behavior. A characteristic early proposition was that males are biochemically katabolic, females, anabolic; thus more congenital criminals are male than female.

In this early period Thomas viewed man mainly as a creature of instinct whose most natural human dispositions were roving, fighting, and hunting. Thomas saw activity which was less spontaneous as irksome, and he held that agriculture and sedentary occupations produced strains in the organism. At an early stage he offered the pursuit of food and sex as the principal motivating forces in the human and perceived society as a confining, artificial, and biologically uncongenial environment. There is perhaps some reflection of this viewpoint in his classification of character types according to the outcome of the struggle between biology and society for control of the individual. In the *bohemian* type the appetites prevailed; the *philistine* conformed to society. The third character type, the *creative man,* may have been invented to provide for a type of nonconformist of which Thomas could approve.

Thomas's early view of social psychology was that it is the study of *individual mental processes* in so far as they are conditioned by society, and the social processes in so far as they are conditioned by states of consciousness. This theory has much closer resemblance to the individualistic conceptions of Floyd Allport than to the more sociological views which were at that time available in the contributions of Dewey, Mead, and Cooley. Although Thomas eventually abandoned the emphasis on instincts and individualism, he never seemed to grasp fully the concept of the person as a *product* of group interaction. He did, however, become more perceptive of social sources of motivation, and this change is well illustrated by his replacing the food-and-sex theory of motivation with the famous four wishes

—recognition, response, new experience, and security—which clearly allow mankind a type of motivation pigs cannot have.[8]

Thomas's writings on the subject of attitudes and values has had far more lasting effect on the course of sociology, and the concern with this topic which he introduced in the early years of the century has spread and expanded, remaining a lively field for research today. Thomas called attention to the relation between attitude and object, or value, and indicated the unitary nature of this connection; the attitude being a mental relation toward some object, and the object itself defined in terms of the attitude. To the extent that men respond to objects, they respond to this kind of defined entity, not to the objective reality of a physical thing.

A similar point was made with reference to the definition of a situation. Persons respond to any complexity of influences with respect to the definition they make of it. The search for specific stimuli defined purely in physical terms as causes of behavior fails by neglecting the part played by attitudes and imagery. In this discussion Thomas was undoubtedly reflecting some conceptions worked out by Dewey and others, whose influence early became part of the atmosphere at Chicago.

An important part of Thomas's work was the continuation of the sociological tradition of exploiting ethnological material. Thomas taught courses in this subject, and in 1909 he published the important *Source Book for Social Origins*, which was required reading for most graduate students at Chicago during the next quarter of a century. Along with Franz Boas, the Columbia University anthropologist, he was among the early writers to elaborate criticisms of theories of racial differences in mental capacity. He also took strong interest in the task of clearing out certain popular nineteenth-century fallacies and errors,

---

[8] For a decade or so this list of four wishes was in vogue among the graduate students at Chicago. Burgess retained a fondness for them long after other sociologists ceased to mention this or any other list of fundamental wishes. Furthermore, he elaborated them into a specific theory, the main point of which held that if a wish in one category, such as a trip abroad for *new experience*, is frustrated, there may be successful substitution of another specific wish in the same category, perhaps scientific research, but that an attempt to substitute a wish in another category, such as *response* or *recognition*, will not succeed. No way of testing these propositions was ever found, and the fashion of listing categories of motivation long ago declined almost to extinction.

destructively criticizing particularism, unilinear evolution, and recapitulation.

After about twenty-five years the *Source Book* was obsolete for classroom use, and Thomas was prevailed upon to undertake a revision. He soon realized that the new book could not have enough similarity to the old to justify the same title. Nevertheless, *Primitive Behavior*, which was published in 1937, was a near-equivalent of the earlier book. Among the eighteen chapters of the second book, Thomas continued to include one entitled "The Relative Mental Endowment of Races," using evidence not from psychological research with mental tests, but from descriptive materials, including proverbs, reflecting the contents of preliterate minds and some of their characteristic ways of reasoning. *Primitive Behavior*, now in its own turn approaching the age of the *Source Book* when a revision was regarded as desirable, remains valuable to the contemporary sociologist as a source collection of instructive ethnographic materials.

A lasting tradition at Chicago was established on the anthropological foundation left by Thomas. An anthropologist, Frederick Starr, joined the department and gave entertaining travelogues to his students for many years. Ellsworth Faris carried on throughout the 1920's the course on Social Origins first organized by Thomas. Ralph Linton and Edward Sapir served in the department for a few years in this period; then Fay Cooper Cole was brought into the department in 1924, and five years later became chairman of a separate department of anthropology. This separation somewhat reduced the responsibility of sociologists for ethnology, but the habit of reading and using ethnological materials remains to this day. In the other direction, the influence of sociology on anthropology remained strong at Chicago, especially through the influence of Robert Redfield, whose training was as much in sociology as in anthropology.

Thomas possessed exceptional physical and mental vigor and greatly surpassed his colleagues in willingness to spend time and energy in gathering abundant material for his research. As early as an 1896 book review, Thomas praised the author for using full and concrete historical evidence rather than relying on speculation and argument, as was common then. His energy was soon called on for his major contribution, with Florian Znaniecki, *The Polish Peasant in Europe and America,* published in five volumes in 1918 and subsequent years. Thomas spent much time in Europe from 1910 to 1918 gathering materials for this study, adding these to data obtained in the United States. He accumulated massive amounts of autobiographical materials, family letters between peasants in Poland and relatives in the United States, newspaper files, public documents, and institutional records.

One volume of the study containing the Methodological Note stands as a major theoretical work by itself. The remaining body of the research contained contributions to the subject of assimilation, the family system, primary group relations, social classes, economic life, religious and magical attitudes, and processes of disorganization and reorganization. Here again there was progress in moving away from the earlier tendency to see matters in terms of individualism, or collective individualism, and to understand sociological processes on their own level and as they influenced the behavior of persons.

The concept of social disorganization introduced in *The Polish Peasant* study is essentially the same as that widely used today, and this introduction served to turn scholars from the humanitarian interest in social problems toward an analysis of the sociological processes of disorganization which cause them.

The general respect sociologists held for *The Polish Peasant* study is indicated by an assessment undertaken by the Social Science Research Council in 1937. When leading sociologists were asked to name the most significant piece of research in American sociology with a view to holding a conference to discuss the chosen work, *The Polish Peasant* study was elected. The conference proceedings began the next year with a lengthy critique by Herbert Blumer, followed by a comment from W. I. Thomas and another by Florian Znaniecki, and continued with a general discussion among the members of the conference.[9]

Blumer's critique was not challenged in any important respect by either Thomas and Znaniecki or by the other members, and hence is probably a fair statement of present judgment on the significance of *The Polish Peasant* in the history of American Sociology. Blumer quoted the authors as having presented their study as an "exemplification of a standpoint and method," rather than as a test or proof of

[9] Herbert Blumer, *Critiques of Research in the Social Sciences: I: An Appraisal of Thomas and Znaniecki's The Polish Peasant in Europe and America* (New York: Social Science Research Council, Bulletin 44, 1939).

hypotheses. He argued effectively that the massive materials on the Poles did not, and could not, constitute a test of any of the propositions of the Methodological Note. Instructive as these descriptive materials may be for showing some aspects of Polish life and the experiences of immigrants, they lack information about the representativeness, adequacy, reliability, and validity of the interpretations provided by the authors. Different readers of the descriptive matter could not achieve independently the same interpretations as those of the authors; moreover, it is clear that the authors did not develop their sociological statements from these data. Thomas acknowledges this discrepancy in the discussion by pointing out that he developed his formulation of the four wishes, not from the Polish observations, but years earlier in 1905. Other important theoretical statements had also been developed earlier, some in Thomas's course in Social Attitudes, and some of the thoughts on values from a volume in Polish by Znaniecki.

Although it was never put this bluntly, it would seem that *The Polish Peasant* consists of two little-related parts. The concrete data on the peasants themselves were but slightly used by the authors and perhaps not at all by any other sociologists; the contribution of this part perhaps was to inspire successors to undertake labor of data gathering on a massive scale. The Methodological Note, on the other hand, which stood apart from the rest of the study, launched an important and enduring discussion of attitudes and values, contributed to the weakening of the instinct theory by the formulation of wishes, and helped to give sociologists the courage, in defiance of the growing vogue of behavioristic psychology, to find a place for subjective aspects of human life. To scholars who were troubled by the problem of whether personal statements could be of use to science in view of the unsolved question of the truth or reality of such statements, Thomas provided the dictum, "If men define situations as real, they are real in their consequences."

If permanent effects of the study are less than were originally hoped for by the authors, they may have taken some satisfaction in the evidence of the spread of their ideas, not only within sociology, but also in neighboring traditions. The handling of immigrants by social workers, for example, is said to have been greatly altered in view of Thomas's notions concerning the phases of disorganization and reorganization experienced by the immigrants—a view far more sophisticated than the earlier conceptions attributing their troubles to biological inferiority. Anthropology was affected in a different way, and anthropologists may have acquired some of their interest in life-history materials, as well as an interest in processes of acculturation, from the example of *The Polish Peasant*.

In his research and teaching, Thomas habitually used the device of noting information on slips of paper which he carried to his classes in his pocket, commenting on the items during his lectures. The separation of gathered knowledge into such small units made possible the fullest freedom of reorganization in his writings, and probably also allowed some insights that could emerge only in the new combinations of materials. For years Ellsworth Faris continued to require all of his students to use the same method in writing their term papers, even requiring them to turn in the slips to make sure they used the method properly.

Although Thomas left the Chicago department in 1919, his prestige remained for many years, and students were more influenced than they realized by his example of active research, his stimulating concepts, and his general approach to the creation of a scientific sociology. His colleagues played their part, but more than any of them, Thomas prepared the ground for the surge of productivity that was to follow soon after the first generation of the Chicago faculty left the campus.

Small stayed only a little longer than Thomas and was far past his prime when he retired in 1923. Informal as well as official leadership of the department was passing into other hands. Small's quarrels with the president of the university reached the point of mutual nonspeaking, and students of the last few years reported his courses to have been unbearably dull. The new department, however, was at this time just entering its decade of highest creativity and its leadership of American sociology.

◄ III ►

The Chicago Background and the New Department

The new discipline of sociology had its most vigorous early growth in a new university in the world's newest large city. Stimulation for creativity permeated the whole Chicago environment of the period, to attract, to support, and perhaps in part to develop the men and the activities needed for the construction of the new science. The newspapers show the city of Chicago amazed at itself from its very beginnings on an unpromising swampy site which contained nothing but a small log fort in 1833. As a result of the rapid westward migration, an important city arose on this site in a scant generation, a city that soon developed a sense of its own destiny to become one of the world's great. The population expansion was spectacular from the beginning, paralleled only by the growth of industry and commerce.

As the West grew and the Midwest matured, Chicago became a favorable center for many kinds of industry, and among the largest of these was the great meat-packing complex. It took a lot of space and spread its odors over many square miles, but it made the city, if not actually "Hog Butcher for the World" as Sandburg's poem bragged, at least the meat market of the central states.

The steel industry next became an important source of income and attracted the laboring population. Ore from the Lake Superior districts came south as far as possible by ship and in South Chicago and nearby Gary, Indiana, joined the bituminous coal coming from the Illinois coalfields by rail. Some of the steel was fabricated there, and among the major users was the Pullman Company, which built the sleeping cars for the American railroads. Other light and heavy industry followed and added to the need for the rest of the complement of businesses and industries needed in any large city. The great wheat exchange also contributed its part to giving the city a considerable amount of financial dominance in the heart of the nation.

About the only thing that could be thought beautiful about late nineteenth–century Chicago was fresh and lively Lake Michigan, a lake which is about as featureless as a large body of water can be, with its low, even shorelines. But civic enthusiasm and a booster spirit demanded some basis for pride. The amazing growth rate and the accompanying rise in land values and the fortunes made from them satisfied some of this demand. Since swift growth produces disorder, there was even some admiration of the very pace of the disorder. From 1850 onward a touch of boasting appeared in the news accounts of Chicago's crime, and by the decade of the 1920's the city claimed the world championship of organized crime. Al Capone, the czar of the underworld, became a celebrity sought out by visitors who desired to take in all the important local sights.

Even the Great Fire of 1871 became a cherished local memory, and schoolchildren were taught that it contributed to the city's greatness by providing the need to rebuild.[1]

Pride was also taken in the claim of having built the first steel-framed skyscraper, in reversing the flow of the Chicago River, and in literally lifting the city up by its bootstraps by jacking up houses in some low sections and pushing dirt under them. Such accomplishments have been made elsewhere, but this fact was not of local significance, and Chicago's feats were taken to be a product of the "I Will" spirit of the city.

Against all the background of stockyard smell and soft-coal soot, however, Chicago had its summer of beauty. Chicago's first World's

[1] The Chicago legend attributes the start of the fire to a lantern kicked over by Mrs. O'Leary's cow. Brass bands in Chicago still like to lead off a concert with the local tune set to words about the event, concluding with "There'll Be a Hot Time in the Old Town Tonight."

Fair, the Columbian Exposition of 1893, was completed a year later than originally intended. A large vacant site on and behind the lake shore was made into a system of parks with a midway, lagoons, groves, and islands and a display of white classical buildings landscaped with heroic statues and fountains. Displays offered modern as well as traditional exhibits, with special featuring of the uses of electricity, then a novelty of great interest.

The Fair was well attended, and visitors from all directions were delighted and impressed. The young Edward Scribner Ames wrote years later, "In the summer of 1893 I visited the World's Fair . . . Against many adverse conditions, including a business depression, the young city of Chicago had created a dream city of such scope and beauty that it brought the world to its gates and displayed the marvels of a new age of invention, of arts, and of communication. The old Field Museum in Jackson Park (later the Museum of Science and Industry), which was the Fine Arts building of the Fair, is an impressive illustration of the architectural grandeur that filled the hundreds of acres along the lake." [2]

As the World's Fair, sometimes remembered as the White City, departed, the two beautiful parks with their improvements, some of the buildings, and the mile long broad Midway with its sunken central strip, remained as permanent civic assets. And as the exposition was closing, along the north side of the Midway the campus of the new University of Chicago was beginning to provide a fresh set of architectural decorations—a replacement celebrated in the third verse of the Alma Mater song, "The City White had fled the earth/ But where the azure waters lie/ A nobler city has its birth/ The City Grey that ne'er shall die."

Previously universities had always grown slowly, evolving sympodially over the course of centuries from the primitive twelfth century models of Bologna and Paris. Many little colleges have, of course, been established outright and some of these have grown in an orderly way into large universities. But only once was a major university established full-blown and ready to take its place at once in the first rank of institutions of higher education. This unprecedented occurrence was the consequence of a remarkable relationship between a man with

[2] Edward Scribner Ames, *Beyond Theology* (Chicago: The University of Chicago Press, 1959), pp. 40–41.

money—John D. Rockefeller—and a man with leadership, inventiveness, and daring—William Rainey Harper.

Rockefeller, already in possession of his great Standard Oil fortune, was much concerned to use some of his wealth for the good of humanity, and during his lifetime gave support to a great range of charitable enterprises. Among his interests was that of education, and the thought came or was suggested to him, of endowing a small college to provide the sort of moral training favored by his theological views. To this end he heard the advice of a fellow Baptist and Yale Professor of Greek and Hebrew, William Rainey Harper. Harper liked the idea and the agreement was made for him to be president and organizer, and soon thereafter he was scouring the country for faculty for the new university to open in the fall of 1892.

Harper had ambitious plans for this university, more than he had initially revealed to Rockefeller. He intended that it should become a university of large size and top quality and quickly committed the donor for funds far beyond the initial endowment gift. By agreement with the trustees the early buildings were placed at the corners of a large quadrangle, rather than in contiguous locations, letting the large gaps speak for themselves. He sought and obtained large gifts from prominent Chicago industrialists, and in cases which required matching funds, sought and obtained some of the required amounts from Rockefeller. Quality and prestige were expressed in the architectural style, limestone Gothic, which in the sooty air of Chicago winters quickly took on the appearance of dignified antiquity. A bit of Oxford atmosphere was achieved by the duplication of Magdalen Tower at the northeast corner of the quadrangle.

Generous publicity by newspapers all over the nation to the development at Chicago resulted in large donations of money and some extensive exhibits from the World's Fair.

If the architectural style of the new university was traditional, little else was. Harper was an innovator and a smasher of academic tradition on a large scale. One of his first and perhaps most important departures from precedent was his establishment of a salary scale about twice that prevailing about the country. These expenditures were made possible by the size of the Rockefeller gifts and were apparently necessary, although not sufficient alone, to attract the original distinguished faculty. Harper had to use all of his gifts of persuasion in the long and hard task of building the first faculty. At one period he came close to discouragement, having worked for months without recruiting a single scholar, but when the task was done, he had secured a faculty universally recognized as great. It was the conviction at Chicago, if not at Harvard and Yale, that from the start this was the best university in the world's history, and whether true or only nearly so, the belief could not help but be a powerful force for intensely high morale at Chicago. Harper brought to his original faculty eight professors who had been college presidents. In this migration of noted scholars to the campus on the Midway it became necessary for Charles Elliott Norton of Harvard to deny that he planned to accept a professorship there. All he had actually said was, "It has grown out of my saying to Dr. James that if I were a younger man I should like to cast my lot with a city like Chicago. I like Chicago. I like the spirit, the civic power of the place."

Other Harper innovations contributed to the dynamic spirit of the university and in many cases to the general academic pattern in the United States as well. The full summer session, for example, was made possible by the novel division of the school year into four quarters, instead of the traditional two semesters separated by a long and idle summer. This device avoids the waste of unused facilities in the summer season and makes possible accelerated progress of students toward degrees. In Harper's quarter system a professor could teach any three of the four quarters each year, or could teach the fourth quarter with extra pay, or could elect to teach for three summer quarters without pay in order to have a full year of paid leave.

Harper is also given credit for instituting extension work in the university pattern. The concept for this came in part from his experience as a lecturer in Chautauqua, in which he held a position of Superintendent of its College of Liberal Arts. Chautauqua extension offered series of lectures to neighborhood clubs and churches, and the extension activity of the university began in the same pattern. Albion Small had also been a Chautauqua lecturer and for a time after his appointment as head of the Department of Sociology at Chicago he continued to lecture in local churches. Later a Downtown College was established in the Chicago Loop, and extension work was systematically offered there for many years.

Less noticed, but equally unprecedented, was Harper's decision to appoint women to the faculty with rank and salaries equal to men with the same duties—an idea far more daring in the 1890's than it is today. He chose to allow the development of intercollegiate football competition, but instead of hiring an itinerant coach for the sole purpose of obtaining victories, he brought in A. A. Stagg to be coach and athletic director and also Professor of Physical Education. Stagg, who had his victories and defeats on the playing fields, spent his entire career at Chicago, leaving only when he reached retirement age, and then turning west for another career. Probably no man has done as much as Stagg to influence collegiate athletic patterns in the direction of honor and sportsmanship and to keep them in harmony with the principal aims of a university.

By no means least of the Harper innovations took place when he called in a scholar of distinction, Albion Small, to found the first department of sociology. It was no accident that the new subject was put into the curriculum in a new organization, unbound by the traditions and vested interests which were to delay the development of sociology in many of the older universities in the Atlantic coast region. When sociology eventually was admitted in these latter institutions, it had to face years of effort to work out of the position of least prestige.

Among the consequences of the immediate high standing of the university was the natural acceptance of research responsibility by the faculty. It was Harper's conception that it is the business of the professor to discover and publish knowledge as much as to teach it in the classroom. But in this highly selected new faculty the responsibility for creation was not mainly a matter of external pressure. The very prominence of the new university carried with it the responsibility for leadership. It was not necessary to ask aloud, Who will create and lead if we do not?

The prevading spirit of creation was further expressed in official symbols. On the University Seal a phoenix arises out of fire. Below it appears the motto *Crescat Scientia, Vita Excolatur*—let science grow that human life be enriched. On the Geology building the thought, carved in stone, is less poetic but equally clear: *Dig and Discover*.

In this supporting atmosphere, then, of vigorous city and exciting new institution, the sociologists, too, were to find encouragement to dig and discover in amounts not customary in the gentler academic atmospheres where ivy sometimes grew faster than knowledge. All these secular supports may have been supplemented by the motivating optimism and selflessness prevailing in nineteenth-century American Protestant theology. As stated before, each of the four members of the sociology faculty at Chicago—Small, Vincent, Henderson, and Thomas—had a background of theological influence, and the same is true of later additions—Burgess and Faris. The wild enthusiasm which not long before had generated a serious intention to Christianize the entire world in a single generation became transferred in these men to the more secular but similarly inspiring aims of higher education and the creation of a new science of social behavior.

These men, Park, Burgess, and Faris, were the nucleus of the organism that was to grow so vigorously in the 1920's. The ground had been cleared by able predecessors—Small, Vincent, and Thomas. The soldiers had returned from the war and were eager for study. The nation was optimistic and the city proud and vigorous. And by no means a minor consideration, large amounts of research money were soon to become available. Sociology was ready to move, and the most rapid movement would be at Chicago.

The transition from the original department at the end of the century may be said to have begun in 1916 with the arrival of Robert Ezra Park, and to be completed in 1923 with the retirement of Albion Small and the appointment of Ellsworth Faris as chairman. The young Ernest W. Burgess also returned in 1916 to become the third member of the nucleus of the new organism.

Burgess was the second product of the departmental training to take a place on the faculty. His doctorate at Chicago was awarded in 1913, with a thesis on *The Function of Socialization in Social Evolution*—a nineteenth-century style of dissertation which did not fully indicate the directions Burgess's productive career was to take. Burgess held successive teaching appointments at Toledo, Kansas, and at Ohio State before returning to the Chicago department in 1916. Although trained in part by Small and Henderson, he soon developed his own interests, and was responsible for developing the sociology of the family and for transforming the fields of social pathology and crime into objective and scientific sociology rather than applied welfare work. His interest and responsibility for sociology as a whole is shown by the fact that for some years, along with Park, he taught the general introductory course, and collaborated with Park on the *Introduction to the Science of Sociology.* This famous textbook, first used by students in mimeographed form, was published in 1921.

Slight of stature, Burgess had the pallor of a man who spent most of his time indoors, in spite of an occasional round of golf on a holiday. Frequently he had a somewhat worn look, well justified by his pace of activity, and a harried appearance, reinforced by a transparent green eyeshade which he wore at his desk and sometimes in the corridors. But he moved quickly and energetically and spoke to his classes in adequate volume. His voice was high and his sentences broken with hesitations, but the knowledge was well-organized and authoritative, and students seldom complained about the style of his lectures.

A lifelong bachelor, Burgess lived with his father and sister in an apartment near the campus. Because of his part in this gentle and affectionate family trio, Burgess never felt unqualified for his teaching and research in the sociology of family life. In fact, as he once explained to a banquet audience of colleagues and students, his bachelorhood provided him with two advantages for family research: objectivity and protection from the temptation to generalize from a single case.

Along with an acknowledged high level of ability, Burgess had an exceptional appetite for work, and few modern sociologists have ever worked as continuously as he.[3] He outlived his colleagues by many years, continuing his productive research all through his years of retirement until it became physically impossible to do so.

Robert E. Park came into academic sociology by a most complex and interesting route. As he told the story himself near the end of his life, it all began with his reading of Goethe.[4] Faust, the aged scholar, felt weary of books and wanted to see the world of men. The young Park, who had completed his undergraduate education at Michigan and become a teacher in Red Wing, Minnesota, made his own Faustian contract with the devil and obtained a newspaper reporter job in Minneapolis. He finished his Minnesota adventure within three years

[3] For example, in about 1933 he planned to take a trip to Russia to obtain materials of sociological interest. He thought it well to acquire some knowledge of the Russian language in advance, but he found no uncommitted time in his daily schedule. His determination led to a solution, however; he purchased language records to be played each morning while he shaved.

[4] Robert E. Park, *Race and Culture* (Glencoe, Illinois: The Free Press, 1950), pp. v–ix, "An Autobiographical Note."

and aimed for the larger world of New York, reaching it by way of jobs in Detroit and Denver. But interest in reporting in New York did not last; Park perceived that this was a young man's game, and that after eight years or so, if a reporter remained in the profession, his value steadily declined.

Park became convinced that the newspaper itself could be a force in history by accurately and adequately reporting important events. He had an appetite for what journalists called big stories—news of basic and long-term significance. Influenced by the exposés of Lincoln Steffens, whose *Shame of the Cities* showed the patterns of urban disorganization and political corruption to be a natural consequence of social forces, Park became fascinated with the sociology of the city. In order to develop his ability to get below the surface of his subject, he returned to school for further study, spending some time in graduate work at Harvard. There he studied philosophy, hoping to gain insight into the nature and function of news, and to learn to describe "the behavior of society, under the influence of news, in the precise and universal language of science."

After a year at Harvard, Park pursued further study abroad at Berlin, Strassburg, and Heidelberg, hearing lectures from Georg Simmel in Berlin and Windelband at Heidelberg and writing his thesis on *Masse und Publikum* under the direction of Windelband. He returned to Harvard in 1903, completing his thesis there, and took an appointment as assistant in philosophy.

Park was soon offered positions in other universities but chose instead to go to Tuskegee to work with Booker T. Washington. Race relations seemed to him to have ever growing importance, and he believed that Washington was able to face the subject with some realism and with less sentimentality than was customary in that period. Thus he spent the next seven years partly at Tuskegee and partly roaming about the South, working as a sort of secretary to Washington and getting acquainted with the life, customs, and situation of the southern Negro. During this period he was also prevailed upon by the secretary of the Baptist Foreign Missions to write a series of articles advertising the atrocities in the Belgian Congo to prepare the way for political reform action. In the process Park learned that the conditions in the Congo were not unique, but that they were what generally takes place "whenever a sophisticated people invades the territories of a more primitive people in order to exploit their lands, and incidentally, to uplift and civilize them."

W. I. Thomas attended a conference at Tuskegee in 1911 and there met Park, who immediately impressed him. This meeting led to an invitation for Park to teach at Chicago in the summer of 1913. The environment was attractive to Park, and he stayed on at Chicago for the rest of his career, learning from and influencing his colleagues in important ways.

Park brought from his newspaper days a general interest in the city. He had written many articles for the Sunday papers and had dealt with many aspects of city life. He claimed, "I expect that I have actually covered more ground, tramping about in cities in different parts of the world, than any other living man. Out of all this I gained, among other things, a conception of the city, the community, and the region, not as a geographical phenomenon merely but as a kind of social organism." Chicago was to provide the opportunity to expand this interest and to give and receive influences from Park's colleagues and students in the department.

Park led a sedentary life and developed a soft and thickset physique. His white hair was long, perhaps more from inattention to visits to the barber than from style preference. He often had the look of the absent-minded professor, and in fact earned it by his characteristic preoccupation. He could on occasion appear before his class with ears full of shaving soap or his clothing out of order. One of his classes in the late 1920's was amused and impressed when he continued his lecture while a student walked to the front of the room and tied Park's neckwear, which had been dangling loose from his collar. Park would frequently forget where he placed a book and even could arrive at a convention forgetting to bring a copy of the paper he was scheduled to read.

Park's voice and manner had a gruff quality that frightened and offended some students. He sometimes felt it desirable to explain to a class that when he frowned or spoke rudely, he did not mean to offend but that this was just his manner when thinking hard. He could and sometimes did tell a student who offered an unsound idea before a class that the thought was not worth a damn, and student tears could flow as a consequence. This gruffness gave offense frequently enough that in the early 1920's there was some resistance to enrolling in Park's courses. Faris found it advisable to have serious talks with graduate students, mostly individually or in small groups, informing them that Park was one of the great scholars in sociology and advising them to take all of his courses and not let his crustiness deprive them of this exceptional opportunity. The advice was widely taken and after a short time it was no longer necessary.

Behind these manners, however, Park was a truly affectionate man, who took much personal interest in his students. He was enormously generous with his time, and tended to adopt his more promising students into something of a protégé status. Park would give such students countless hours of private conversation in the course of which he would all but supply them with the framework of a dissertation or even a book. Few of his students have been able adequately to acknowledge the extent of their personal debt to Park, for he gave them organized sociology in such a way that it came to appear to them as their own.

Park not only gave organization to the sociology he offered to the students, but he also stimulated their extensive exploratory activity. He successfully exhorted them to seek rich personal experience with the topics of their interest; to get inside of the subject and even live it as far as possible. Often he would go along with a student on a search for material to provide an example of how to go about it. Thus did the former philosopher and newspaper man bring new dimensions to the research training of sociology students at Chicago.

The pathway to Chicago and sociology taken by Ellsworth Faris was even more indirect. His college course trained him to be an engineer, but youthful idealism influenced him to become a missionary. After seven years in Africa his health became temporarily impaired, so he returned to Texas and soon took an appointment at Texas Christian University, a church-affiliated college then located in Waco, teaching theology and philosophy. After a few years he decided to improve himself and at considerable effort went to the University of Chicago, taking along his wife and four children, and there embarked on the long course of training for a doctorate in the department of philosophy. Influenced by his teachers, John Dewey and George H. Mead, he found his interest in theology declining and an interest in psychology growing. He therefore completed his degree in the field of psychology and taught in the Department of Psychology at Iowa for several years.

He moved to the University of Chicago in 1919 and only then transferred his responsibilities to the field of sociology.

A trivial accident is connected with the offer of an appointment in sociology at Chicago. Faris had been invited to talk on "The Mental Capacity of Savages" before a faculty and graduate student group in the Chicago department of sociology. A graduate student forgot his assigned duty to send the information to the university calendar which carried announcements of meetings and in remorse sought help from the faculty when he foresaw the visiting scholar arriving to talk with no audience on hand. Since it was too late to do anything else, the faculty persuaded a number of influential professors in other departments, along with some members of the administration, to constitute a small but important audience. It was this group which was favorably impressed by the talk and well-disposed to the appointment of Faris at the time of Thomas's departure. Thomas had been regularly offering instruction in social psychology, and, since the Department of Psychology itself was not strong at the time, it was appropriate to add Faris from that field, especially in view of his training in the Dewey-Mead tradition and his known broad interest in ethnological subjects, resulting in part from his experiences in Africa.

Faris was a six-foot, 185 pound vigorous former athlete. He had been a natural leader in his boyhood and during his youthful missionary years and retained a dominant manner in his relations with students and to some extent with colleagues. His well-organized lectures were presented in a clear, full voice and often somewhat dramatically delivered, partly retaining the quality of the sermons he was experienced in delivering. He enjoyed his large classes and sensed the lively response from the student audiences. He also had a general fondness for students and for certain protégés in particular, but he could also clash with an overconfident student. He did not like to be interrupted or to have a point challenged during a lecture and would on some occasions lash out with cutting sarcasm. Once during a discussion of introversion a student raised a hand to ask if Faris meant to imply that there was anything undesirable about being introverted. The sharp reply, "No, go right on," caused the student to transfer to another academic department.

Faris taught for four quarters a year during most of his career at Chicago, and sometimes he taught extension courses at the downtown college as well. He gave a great deal of time and attention to his administrative duties and to the support of the work of his colleagues, as well as to the maintenance of morale in the department. He published little; some forty articles and a number of book reviews constitute his scholarly record. He considered his major achievement to be the support of the conditions which made the department as a whole the effective instrument it was for education and the production of new knowledge.

These three men, Park, Burgess, and Faris, along with the now wearying Small, were the regular departmental faculty at Chicago in 1920. There was also an instructor, Scott Bedford, who did not stay much longer, and a number of advanced graduate students who did some teaching in the introductory course—among these in the early 1920's were Louis Wirth, Herbert Blumer, Carl Dawson, E. T. Krueger, Frederic Thrasher, and Eyler N. Simpson. In addition to these men, the department of the 1920's lists Nels Anderson, Clifford Shaw, Walter Reckless, Andrew Lind, Ernest Mowrer, William Byron, Harry Sell, E. H. Shideler, John H. Mueller, Samuel Kincheloe, Erle Fisk Young, Norman Hayner, Ruth Shonle, George Vold, Willard Waller, Helen MacGill, Harvey Zorbaugh, L. Guy Brown, Floyd House, Charles S. Johnson, Jesse F. Steiner, R. D. McKenzie, Earl Johnson, Robert Redfield, Everett Stonequist, E. T. Hiller, Fay B. Karpf, Leslie A. White, Martin H. Neumeyer, Thomas C. McCormick, Samuel A. Stouffer, Carl M. Rosenquist, Howard Paul Becker, James A. Quinn, E. Franklin Frazier, Carroll D. Clark, Edgar T. Thomson, Philip M. Hauser, Richard A. Lang, John Dollard, Paul G. Cressey, Paul F. Cressey, Ellen Black, Clarence Glick, and others whose names have since become familiar to students of sociology.

This was the early postwar period, when universities in general had a great enrollment surge in both undergraduate and graduate schools. The war veterans, mature and accustomed to working, came in large numbers, some with partial support from the government. This was a new breed of graduate student, easy to teach and enthusiastic for sociology and for the academic career. The general level of morale in this student body was high. They had come to this department with the conviction that it was "*the* place to go"; some adding that, "the other place was Columbia."

Until the Social Science building was erected in 1929, the offices and most of the classes in the department were in the Harper Memorial Library, the most impressive and also the most convenient building on the large campus. A towered fortress dominating the Midway on the south side of the central quadrangle, this building held the president's office, the main library and great reading room, ample classroom, and offices for several departments. Faris had a small office on the top floor of the east tower, and Park and Burgess shared a room on a lower floor. For a time the office of the *American Journal of Sociology* was in a tight space designed as a broom closet. The atmosphere of compression and urgency, in a setting of gothic dignity, seemed at the time suitable for pursuing scholarly objectives. New students often expressed a feeling of excitement at the environment, the faculty, their fellow-students, and the sense of movement in the field of sociology. They were aware that new sociology was being built, and that they were at the center of its development. Their teachers worked long hours, and it was a matter of course for most of the graduate students to do the same. For those who learned how, it meant rapid progress toward a degree. Norman S. Hayner, for example, recorded in his personal diary for 1921 the following items:

Feb. 9. Worked out plan for thesis. [M.A. thesis]
May 3. Handed in thesis.
May 9. Interview with Burgess. Must reorganize my entire thesis.
May 11. Worked out a better outline for my thesis.
May 22. Must rewrite conclusions.
June 3. Delivered three copies of thesis to library.

By no means all of the instruction was in the classrooms. In addition to the usual discussions among students and office conversations with professors, there were also special committees and organizations within the department membership. Hayner's diary refers to a meeting of the Society for Social Research on January 13, 1921, at which there was a report by Park on the Section on Research of the American Sociological Society, a paper by Galpin on research on towns, and some words from Charles E. Merriam of the Department of Political Science. On February 3, 1921, there was a meeting of the Sociology Club with a talk from a Professor Wittbank on "Psychoanalysis," which turned out to be a summary of arguments against Freud. On March 25 of the same year Hayner attended sessions of the Western Division of the American Psychological Association at which he heard a paper by Ellsworth Faris, "Are Instincts Data or Hypotheses?" and a paper by George H. Mead. There were other special committees and unorganized meetings, and during this period there were also formed two quasi-fraternal organizations of graduate students, Zeta Phi and Sigma Theta.

Zeta Phi was the first to be formed on the initiative taken by Ernest T. Krueger. Faris had early word of the move and opposed it, believing that such an organized elite within the student group would have a divisive effect, harmful to morale. Krueger persisted, and the result was permanent bad feeling between them.

Zeta Phi had only male members and used a somewhat florid initiation ritual for its first few years, until a later generation discarded it. Sigma Theta included women. Although neither had an oath of exclusive loyalty, by some kind of unspoken custom a student did not belong to both. For all of this imitation of the Greek letter organizations for undergraduates, both societies held regular meetings with speakers and discussions of much educational value.

The mutual respect among the related departments at Chicago also led to valuable enrichment. Hayner's diary records lectures from James Westfall Thompson of the History Department, George Herbert Mead and Edward Scribner Ames of Philosophy, Harvey Carr of Psychology, Harold Lasswell of Political Science, Charles H. Judd of the School of Education, and Edward Sapir of Anthropology. It was common also to take courses in other departments, and statistical instruction was regularly taken in the Economics Department before the arrival of William F. Ogburn in 1927.

Nor was there concentration on hearing only Chicago scholars. Edward A. Ross, who had taught in the 1897 summer term at Chicago, gave a talk in 1921 to the students in the department, and many other visiting scholars appeared from time to time. Graduate students were also expected to know something of all the sociological traditions, not only in the United States but in Europe as well. Everett Hughes has recalled (in a personal communication) that in the seminars he attended in 1923 the students read Pareto's *Treatise on General Sociology* in French (it had not yet been translated into English), and much of Durkheim, Simmel, Weber, von Wiese, Mauss, Vaihinger, and others, in their original languages. Hughes remembers that some students had to struggle with these writings, perhaps motivated to read them mainly by the language requirement for the doctorate, but he recalls that the more ambitious students, including Wirth, Blumer, and Redfield among others, took the reading of these works seriously, more for the ideas than as preparation for examinations.[5] These students formed a natural leadership group among their fellows and helped to set the standards of aspiration for knowledge.

As Fay Karpf has put it, this avoidance of a commitment to single doctrine is associated with the ripening of a field of knowledge: "When a science is sufficiently mature and advanced to have a clear conception of its problems and is able to organize its forces so as to attract them effectively, there are no schools. Schools of psychology are the growing pains of the science. Leaders of the schools perform the same function as fanatics in any sphere. The fanatic in religious or political or social life is one who calls attention to a neglected truth or duty by a strident exaggeration of its importance. They not only tend to become extremists, but they are also in danger of losing their scientific temper, since the search for truth is suspended by the necessity for fighting." [6]

The emphasis on objectivity became firmly established at Chicago by the early 1920's. As mentioned earlier, Small was partly responsible for this stress, and Thomas as well. Faris, in spite of his early preacher-missionary background, had absorbed the spirit of science in his training in psychology and strongly supported the commitment to objectivity all through his career in sociology. Park was probably the only one who directly attacked the humanitarian attitude when it appeared among sociologists. More than once he drove students to anger or tears by growling such reproofs as, "You're another one of those damn do-gooders."

Years later, after his retirement, Burgess spoke of the fruit the early

[5] Today such diverse reading would probably be a matter of course for leading departments, but in the earlier period when schools of thought contended for followers, students were sometimes expected to learn from the one true source, or at least from readings harmonious with it. A sociologist trained by Ward and his disciple Dealey in his later years complained with some bitterness that those teachers never directed his attention to the leading sociological works in other traditions widely known outside of Brown University. There is also some tendency to recall a similar confinement of attention by students of the Sumner-Keller tradition. This pattern was also strongly prevalent in much of European sociology.

[6] Fay Berger Karpf, *American Social Psychology* (New York: McGraw-Hill Book Co., 1932), p. xvi.

spirit of objectivity had borne: "The discovery that the ethnic community was a gigantic sociological defense mechanism which facilitated the survival and adjustment of immigrants but which the second
generation sought to modify and escape was a major research accomplishment of urban sociology during the 1920's and 1930's. Because it was a heated public issue, and because ethnic neighborhoods
in the city were colorful and distinctive in their variety, sociologists
were fascinated by urban ethnological research. Almost none of this
work was solely descriptive, in the tradition of folk anthropology of
the time. Instead, it was analytical and concentrated on exploring
the behavior patterns and processes of adjustment and change as the
immigrant adapted to the new economic environment. . . . Hostility
and tension between ethnic groups were treated as objective phenomena to be explained, rather than a battle to be joined." [7]

[7] Ernest W. Burgess and Donald J. Bogue, *Contributions to Urban Sociology*
(Chicago: University of Chicago Press, 1964), p. 325.

The Park and Burgess Text

Introduction to the Science of Sociology, the famous textbook written by Park and Burgess, has been thought by many sociologists to have been one of the most influential works ever written in sociology. This contention is based partly on the observation that before its publication in 1921, general treatises on sociology were so variable in content that they had little in common. After the Park and Burgess book, and presumably to a considerable extent because of it, there was a reasonably adequate standardization of the subject. Thus sociology today has a recognizable connection with this book in a way that it does not have with works of the prominent earlier American writers— Small, Ross, Giddings, and Ward. The direction and content of American sociology after 1921 was mainly set by the Park and Burgess text.

Furthermore, it is entirely reasonable to suppose that this book constituted a major contribution to the research impetus that followed so soon on its publication. Earlier works in the field of sociology contained suggestions which could be followed up, but none gave the basis for such a wide range of sociological interest. William G. Sumner's *Folkways*, for example, suggests possibilities of exploring variations, origins, and changes of customs, and some generalizations on institutions. Franklin H. Giddings's writings may have stimulated some work on social motivation and small group formation and possibly some broad speculation on evolution. Lester F. Ward's writings seem not to have fostered much research of any kind, and the Herbert Spencer tradition played out in a relatively brief time. The fourteen chapters of the Park and Burgess text, however, contain a framework for sociological treatment of human nature and personality, group formation, interaction processes, organization, social forces, social change, and in fact almost all of the range of interests that may be found among sociologists today. The existence of this work in the hands of young research students gave meaning and a possible place in a broad unified theory for proposed research topics of a great many kinds. The book provided a sense of proper territory for sociology so that one could work with some degree of confidence that his interests belonged in the field and his research would yield findings that could be cumulative and organized.

The book grew in part out of the introductory course in sociology taught by both Park and Burgess before 1920. Former students recall an apparently trivial occurrence that may have supplied the final impulse to the authors. It is said that another instructor teaching the same course had a considerable amount of mimeographed material in lieu of a text which he sold to the students for personal gain. Complaints from students stimulated Park and Burgess to produce a regular text. It could hardly be supposed, however, that without this incident the book would not have been written. Park especially was frequently set in motion by minor irritations. Although his touchiness often gave rise to productive results, he did not wait for his emotions to push him to work.

Without in any way depreciating the work of Burgess, it must be recognized that Park was the senior member of the pair and made the more definitive contribution to the book's systematic character. Behind both authors was the thinking and example of W. I. Thomas, to whom they expressly state their indebtedness "for the point of view and the scheme of organization of materials which have been largely adopted in this book." In particular, they imply drawing from Thomas's *Source Book for Social Origins* (1909). But while the inspiration of Thomas must indeed have been significant, the Park and Burgess achievement was much greater; their text made a longer stride forward in general sociology than did the *Source Book*, or for that matter any previous sociological work in the United States.

The originality of the book, as is generally the case in such works, lies principally in the assembly and organization of material. It is difficult to find a completely new idea in sociology at any time because from prehistoric times onward all peoples have been experiencing applied sociology in their daily lives and have been at least informally generalizing on this experience. The success of a new general work depends on the selection of sound elements and the statement of these in a valuable systematic form, all having reasonable connections with organized evidence or research activity.

Here Park's personal dispositions came usefully into play. Throughout the earlier stages of his career, as previously indicated, he had the philosopher's disposition to search for larger principles, to organize and generalize, to look for the big stories not only in journalism but also in broader fields, and with even greater persistence in sociology. He was always in a hurry and wanted amounts of organized knowledge greater than one man could gather in a lifetime. He was not too impatient to sit down at a desk and work, but he preferred large-scale discovery and ever expanding generalization to intensive research on a narrow subject. This preference disposed him to work in and through other persons and to collaborate with students in a most generous style in which he supplied ideas at length and allowed the students to get much of the credit for the research achievements that followed. Park also liked to talk all around a subject, usually at great length, with colleagues and students.

In recalling the flavor of such conversations Burgess says: "I returned to Chicago to join the staff in 1916. . . . It was my good fortune to be placed in the same office with Dr. Park. . . . and we began a collaboration that continued as long as he was at the University of Chicago. Our office arrangement was most fortunate for me, because Dr. Park had a most creative mind. He lived and slept research. I never knew when I would get home for dinner, because we would spend whole afternoons discussing both theoretical and practical aspects of sociology and social research." [1] (Park also did not know when he would be home for dinner, and family resentment of his irregular schedule is remembered by his children to this day.)

One of the most important decisions relating to the proposed textbook was to make explicit and conspicuous a commitment to science

[1] Ernest W. Burgess and Donald J. Bogue, *Contributions to Urban Sociology* (Chicago: University of Chicago Press, 1964), p. 3.

by adopting the title *Introduction to the Science of Sociology.* Later texts could afford to use briefer titles, omitting the word *science,* because of this precedent.

It must be supposed that Park, rather than Burgess, who never fully suppressed his active humanitarianism, is responsible for writing: "Sociology seems now, however, in a way to become, in some fashion or other, an experimental science. It will become so as soon as it can state existing problems in such a way that the results in one case will demonstrate what can and should be done in another. Experiments are going on in every field of social life, in industry, in politics, and in religion. In all these fields men are guided by some implicit or explicit theory of the situation, but this theory is not often stated in the form of a hypothesis and subjected to a test of the negative instances. We have, if it is permitted to make a distinction between them, investigation rather than research." [2]

Although Park always openly scoffed at do-gooders in conversation, he wrote more tactfully in the book, quoting *The Polish Peasant* for this purpose: "The oldest but most persistent form of social technique is that of 'ordering-and-forbidding'—that is, meeting a crisis by an arbitrary act of will decreeing the disappearance of the undesirable or the appearance of the desirable phenomena, and the using of arbitrary physical action to enforce the decree. This method corresponds exactly to the magical phase of natural technique." [3]

The Thomas example was followed in another important respect— that of recognizing the importance of research based on active investigation. To influence students in this direction, the text specifically instructed: "The first thing that students in sociology need to learn is to observe and record their own observations; to read, and then to select and record the materials which are the fruits of their readings; to organize and use, in short, their own experience. The whole organization of this volume may be taken as an illustration of the method, at once tentative and experimental, for the collection, classification, and interpretation of materials, and should be used by students from the very outset in all their reading and study." [4]

[2] Robert Ezra Park and Ernest W. Burgess, *Introduction to the Science of Sociology* (Chicago: University of Chicago Press, 1921), p. 45.
[3] *Ibid.,* p. 47.   [4] *Ibid.,* pp. v–vi.

The authors saw the search for knowledge as the task before them, and applications for human welfare were taken as useful only after such knowledge became adequate.

The Park and Burgess text was widely read and used by sociologists at other universities, as well as in the introductory sociology course offered to sophomores at the University of Chicago. Burgess regularly gave an introductory sociology course for graduate students in which he also used the text. Since there was no rule against receiving credit for this graduate course even if a student had already taken introductory sociology in his undergraduate years, a student sometimes had two courses based on the Park and Burgess text and might find the second time as instructive as the first.

From the beginning of the department Small and Thomas had recognized that the grand theorizing of Spencer, Ward, and others would not build a sound tradition of sociology. But there were sensible statements from Europe to draw on, and Thomas, as well as Park after him, had thoughts of his own. Out of the various streams of influence, Park assembled a statement of the proper field for sociology which can be severely summarized in the following statement: *Sociology is the pursuit of objective scientific knowledge concerning the nature of society and social organization, groups, and institutions, the nature and effects of processes of social interaction, and the effects of these forms and processes on the behavior of persons.* This formulation, with inevitable minor variations and elaborations, usefully continues to define the field of sociology today, not only in the United States, but widely about the world. The two chief rivals to this statement are perhaps the tendency to see sociology as grand reform concepts for abolishing social evils, a view destined by its emotional content to remain fractionated into a variety of cults; and doctrinaire Marxian sociology, which can only evolve into a declining exercise in tortured exegesis.

In Chapter I of their textbook Park and Burgess provide a review which indicates that the central problem of sociology had been a matter of interest as long ago as the time of Aristotle. They write of it as the fundamental problem of social control which asks: "How does a mere collection of individuals succeed in acting in a corporate and consistent way? How in the case of specific types of social group, for example an animal herd, a boys' gang, or a political party, does the group control its individual members; the whole dominate the parts?" [5]

Aristotle's answer was too glib to be useful—groups held together because of the innate character of man the political animal. He held that man was made for life in society just as the bee is made for life in the hive. Society is merely the natural and inevitable consequence.

Thomas Hobbes offered a contrasting view, one of a human nature opposed to collective life, with a war of each against all as the most direct expectation relating to the dispositions of man. In his view society could only arise by a general consent among men for mutual protection against one another.

W. Trotter, writing in the period when the instinct theory had its greatest vogue, contrived an explanation on the basis of a supposed herd instinct which would account for human behavior in the same way that it explained the actions of sheep. As he saw it, man is gregarious because of his homogeneity and sensitivity to the behavior of his fellows. Anyone who is otherwise tends to be eliminated by natural selection, as is the sheep which strays from the flock and is eaten by wolves. The strongest instinct thus is to be in and remain with the herd, and conscience, public opinion, and authority are based on such a disposition to conform to the ways of the herd. [6]

The explanation offered by Giddings was somewhat similar, but it avoided the concept of instinct in favor of his own theory of like-mindedness. Creatures who respond alike to like stimuli achieve a basis for cooperation, and to Giddings this appeared to be the only possible basis. As he put it: "I have attempted to show that in like response to the same given stimulus we have the beginning, the absolute origin, of all concerted activity—the inception of every conceivable form of cooperation; while in unlike response, and in unequal response, we have the beginning of all those processes of individuation, of differentiation, of competition, which in their endlessly varied relations to combination, to cooperation, bring about the infinite complexity of organized social life." [7]

[5] *Ibid.*, p. 27.

[6] W. Trotter, *Instincts of the Herd in Peace and War* (New York, 1916), pp. 29–30.

[7] Franklin H. Giddings, *The Concepts and Methods of Sociology* (Congress of Arts and Science, Universal Exposition: St. Louis, 1904), p. 789.

Gabriel Tarde's concept of imitation played a similar service, but as he saw it, men become like-minded by imitation, not because they are born that way. Agreement of minds and wills is necessary to social life, and this comes from the process in which an idea or act spreads from one person to another through suggestion-imitation.

In all of the above attempts to explain the sociability of man, the focus of interest was on similarity or identity of behavior. Society was seen as based on some principle which caused men to behave alike and to be aware of, and perhaps even to cherish, the likeness. It remained to Émile Durkheim to break through a serious limitation in such reasoning and to explain the existence also of social bonds based on complementary differences. In doing so, he also pulled free of the limiting nominalism of all of the foregoing writers, who explained all social phenomena solely in terms of individual characteristics.

Durkheim argued that men may act together not only on the basis of similar purposes but also because of a *common purpose*, which may produce a group which has a real corporate existence of its own, with characteristics and properties that are *sui generis*—and not the sum of, or even like, the characteristics of the individuals which compose the group. This group may then control its own members and cause them to be different from what they were before taking their places in it. Such a group, involving the principle of division of labor, may operate to achieve a common purpose without making its members like-minded or alike in behavior, and in fact is more likely to have the effect of producing individual diversity.

Durkheim was not unaware that groups may form on the basis of similarities among the members; his contribution was to perceive that an important amount of human social behavior is also based on the corporate form of organization, on *complementary differences*. He withdrew from the futile quest for a single principle to account for the social life of man and elaborated the now prevailing conception of the two kinds of social ties—mechanical solidarity and organic solidarity, sharing this conceptualization with other theorists of his time, including Henry Maine and Ferdinand Tönnies, who offered closely parallel thoughts expressed in different terminology.

Neither Park nor Burgess had strong qualifications in social psychology, and in their treatment of this subject they could hardly be expected to be far ahead of their times. But as sociologists, they had to take account of the material society has to work with. Animals have far fewer organized interrelations, and the most elaborate of nonhuman societies—those of the social insects—operate on principles entirely different from those in human societies.

In the early part of the chapter on "Human Nature," the authors present a key quotation from Cooley, establishing a firm sociological groundwork for the whole chapter: ". . . human nature comes into existence. Man does not have it at birth; he cannot acquire it except through fellowship, and it decays in isolation." [8] Here the dependence on the nineteenth-century hereditarian bias is cleanly cut, never to be successfully reestablished in sociology. Attention is thus turned to interaction processes and roles and to the phenomenon of the self-concept as expressed by Cooley: [The reflected or looking-glass self] "seems to have three principal elements: the imagination of our appearance to the other person, the imagination of his judgment of that appearance, and some sort of self-feeling, such as pride or mortification. The comparison with a looking-glass hardly suggests the second element, the imagined judgment, which is quite essential. The thing that moves us to pride or shame is not the mere mechanical reflection of ourselves, but an imputed sentiment, the imagined effect of this reflection upon another's mind." [9]

Park takes this theme in his own words, quoting from an earlier book: "Man is not born human. It is only slowly and laboriously, in fruitful contact, cooperation, and conflict with his fellows, that he attains the distinctive qualities of human nature." [10] The theme has its full elaboration in Chapters III and IV, dealing with "Society and the Group" and "Isolation," but to some extent it is treated throughout the book.

Park, following Durkheim and others, elected to view the organic unity of society as having two bases. Well aware of the three sets of paired terms used by Durkheim, Maine, and Tönnies, Park nevertheless preferred to employ English terms to make the distinction. For a time he wrote and spoke of *community* and *society*, with meanings essentially similar to the Tönnies *Gemeinschaft* and *Gesellschaft*, but

[8] Charles H. Cooley, *Social Organization*, 1909, p. 30.
[9] Charles H. Cooley, *Human Nature and the Social Order*, 1902, pp. 152–153.
[10] Robert E. Park, *Principles of Human Behavior*, (New York: Zolaz, 1915), p. 9.

in the long run he seemed to prefer *symbiosis* and *consensus,* the concepts used in the Introduction.

The term *symbiosis* was borrowed from ecology where it designates patterns of competitive relations based on the universal unintentional struggle for survival and it yields simple and elaborate, as well as stable, forms of cooperation among like and different species. A simple form of such unwitting competitive cooperation is illustrated by the oak and the moss, which are associated because of mutual benefits; the oak providing favorable shade to the moss, and the moss conserving water for the oak's use. Elaborate examples are found in such biotic communities as an old swamp or a mature forest, in which a great variety of plants and animals constitute such an ecological unity that many, if not all, of the living creatures contribute to the survival of some or all of the others and produce a lasting complex organization of living things. Park's transfer of the term *symbiosis* to sociology was clearly meant to be an analogy to demonstrate that some types of elaborate organization of human interrelations may arise from purely competitive forces, with no necessity of consciousness or intention playing any part.

Although human society involves *consensus* (the second term) as animal and plant societies cannot, Park argued that it would also be worthwhile to study the symbiotic aspects of human life. Man competes with animals and plants, as well as with other men, for survival, and his behavior and form of social activity are affected by his place in the entire world of living things. In addition, among his fellows man competes in many ways without intending to and often without knowing it. He can never, in fact, fully realize the effects of his simple acts of purchasing and consuming on other persons in the grand web of life. A consumer in Oregon buying a pair of nylon socks at a store differentially influences the welfare of a cotton sharecropper in Georgia and a retired shareholder in Vermont, without either knowing or intending such effects. The web of competitive relations among humans can also attain something of an organic character, and Park was particularly interested in the promise of human ecology in accounting for some of the features of the great metropolis, where human competition reaches its highest intensities.

Park sometimes spoke of human ecology as the "attempt to isolate the symbiotic element in human life." He never failed to make clear that this was only a conceptual isolation, and that in real life it is difficult or impossible to find ecological patterns of human behavior completely unadulterated by the consensus element. *Human ecology* was thus offered as a sort of ideal concept—similar to those of the perfect market or economic man—which do not exist, although approximations of each may be usefully studied.

Consensus relations are presented only sketchily in the chapter that deals with symbiosis, but they are discussed sufficiently to indicate the character of that other, and actually main, aspect of sociology. Communication and the consensus concept are developed in an apt passage from Durkheim, showing the respect in which "collective representations" are literally collective, having a life longer and wider than that of any of the individual persons who must be the bearers of such elements of culture. Thus a language, which in one sense can exist only in individuals, has an organized structure which need not have been devised by any one person, or even intended by any. It has a life far longer than any living generation and grows and changes according to principles that can hardly be imagined to emerge from individual minds. For particular persons, it comes to them from outside and forces them to conform (in their language behavior) to its nature.

Such is the nature of all collective representations and of culture itself. Nothing mystical need be asserted, and Durkheim specifically renounced mystical implications, as Park and Burgess would have done if they had felt the need to do so.

The chapter entitled "Isolation" serves to support the earlier chapter on human nature through observation of the consequences of inadequate social experience. In general, the fragmentary evidence presented in this chapter is consistent with the thesis that various degrees of deprivation of social participation are associated with degrees of deficiency in human nature. Although the materials are crude, such additional knowledge as has been accumulated in the succeeding forty-five years continues to support this proposition.[11]

[11] The most severe casualty among the quoted materials was the brief section on feral men, quoted from an earlier survey by Maurice Small and published in 1900 in *Pedagogical Seminary*. Here Caspar Hauser, the Hessian Boy, the Irish Boy, the Lithuanian Boys, the Girl of Cranenburg, Clemens of Overdyke, Jean de Liège, the Savage of Aveyron, Peter of Hanover, the Savage of Kronstadt, the Girl of Songi, and the Wolf Children of India I were introduced to the world of

The entire treatment of human nature in the Park and Burgess book satisfactorily supported the main theme—human nature is a product of social living. Sociology was thereby freed from the excessive and unrewarding dependence regarding this subject on specialists in the field of biology. The hereditarian bias and instinctivism did not die out abruptly, however, and both Park and Burgess made transitional compromises with nineteenth-century doctrines on these subjects, drawing on writings by such men as Edward L. Thorndike, Théodule A. Ribot, Morton Prince, and Charles B. Davenport. Even Park, in a discussion of racial temperament (pp. 138 ff.), speaks of "distinctive characteristics, determined by physical organizations and transmitted biologically. These characteristics manifest themselves in a genial, sunny, and social disposition . . . for expression rather than enterprise and action." But such items were only fading vestiges of a Darwinian dominance of social theory, inconsistent with the sociological contributions of the Park and Burgess text.

Isolation is a factor in determining the character of societies and nations, as well as individuals, and its effects are somewhat parallel. For this reason the authors included some well-known contributions, partly from human geography, of the connections between isolation and national individuality.

The chapter entitled "Social Contacts" presented some classifications of types of relationship contributed by various writers. Sumner's distinction between *in-group* and *out-group relations* and the familiar contrast of *primary* and *secondary contacts* are among these.

A brief statement, adapted from a book by N. S. Shaler, *The Neighbor,* presented the categories of *sympathetic contacts* and *categoric contacts.* In discussing categoric contacts Shaler invited the reader to consider what takes place when two strangers meet. Knowing little or nothing about each other, they are forced to make judgments based on indications of categories. Each is taken as a member of a group, a class, or a type, and dealt with accordingly, even though each may be unaware of the act of categorizing.

---

sociological scholarship. They have all dropped out of the literature, and their successors, the Wolf Children II, and for that matter even later Wolf Children of India, always stay well out of reach of scientific investigation. There is no good reason to suppose that a wolf ever successfully adopted a human infant, but the feral man myths seem to satisfy an appetite that occurs even among scholars.

Sympathetic contacts, on the other hand, involve the understanding of the other person as a unique individual, sharing many characteristics of the person making the contact. To quote the text (p. 297): "When, as in the sympathetic state, we feel that the neighbor of our species is essentially like ourself, the tacit assumption is that his needs and feelings are as like our own as our own states of mind at diverse times are like one another, so that we might exchange motives with him without experiencing any great sense of strangeness." One might compare this point with a distinction introduced much later between relations which have been called *universalistic* and *particularistic*.

Social interaction was presented in a separate chapter, and Park intended the term interaction to have the same meaning in sociology as in other sciences. Indeed, the concept is first presented in a quotation from the field of physics in which the interaction of billiard balls is used to illustrate not merely the effect of one object on another, but the internal modifiability of the two objects as well. The materials on social interaction emphasize the role played by communication through gesture, sympathy, imitation, suggestion, and language. The reciprocal influencing of the interacting persons is clearly stated.[12]

The final eight chapters of the text, considered by some admirers as the heart of the book, treat extensively the major social processes under the chapter headings of "Social Forces," "Competition," "Conflict," "Accommodation," "Assimilation," "Social Control," "Collective Behavior," and "Progress." The abundance of material from Simmel in this part of the book indicates the major influence he had on the thinking of Park.

The *social forces* concept presented materials on public opinion, interests, sentiments, and attitudes, as well as the post-instinct attempts at classifying human motives, and included "The Freudian Wish," a topic which perhaps needed to be mentioned in any book that wished to be thought modern then. The still-born six interests suggested by Albion Small and the somewhat more popular and lasting four wishes of W. I. Thomas were also outlined.

The treatment of *competition* continued the discussion of human ecology first introduced in Chapter III and added materials on some

---

[12] In recent times a vogue has arisen for using *transaction* for the same meaning. The replacement has been justified by a contention that *interaction* does not connote reciprocal influence.

outcomes of competitive processes, including migration, segregation, and selection. Populations that lose most heavily in the universal competition were described in a passage on *inner enemies*—the defectives, the dependents, and the delinquents (designations taken from Henderson's teachings, which influenced Burgess).

Conflict processes included war, political interaction, rivalry, gangs, sects, and race and labor conflicts. These terminated in such *accommodation* processes as compromise, treaty, slavery, caste, and class, and sometimes in conditions of *assimilation*, which differs from accommodation in that in the former differences disappear altogether and the conflicting populations become one.

Park viewed the four chapters on competition, conflict, accommodation, and assimilation as representing one natural progression of an experience of peoples. Competitive relations sometimes lead to conflict, which may be reduced first by accommodation and finally terminated by assimilation, a succession of experiences supposed to have occurred in various times and regions. This was also the framework in which Park thought it profitable to view the experiences of many immigrant populations in the United States.

The final chapters deal with "Social Control" (law, institutions, public opinion, myth and ceremony, religion, newspapers, propaganda, and such topics), "Collective Behavior" (the cycle of social movements and revolutions), and "Progress" (the prospect of control through scientific knowledge, including sociology). The concept of progress of course is entangled with the values of the persons who use it, and values are always in a state of controversy and revision. As an example (p. 1002), a prominent statistician's 1913 list of indices of progress gave: (1) Increase in population, (2) Length of life, (3) Uniformity in population, (4) Racial homogeneity, (5) Literacy, and (6) Decrease in the divorce rate.

Park's comment on the above list included the observation, not likely to be challenged after the passage of a half century, "Certainly these indices . . . are mere temporary measures of progress." And in the closing sentence of the book, "From the point of view of social research the problem of progress is mainly one of getting devices that will measure all the different factors of progress and of estimating the relative value of different factors in the progress of the community."

If the leading sociologists of that early post-war time could not clarify the nature of progress, we may be willing to admit that the concept continues to trouble us today. Yet many modern sociologists would share Park's general viewpoint that the human race is more likely to achieve whatever it wants if we succeed in building up enough useful knowledge of human nature and society to match that which has given us such impressive control of physical nature.

~⦙ IV ⦙~

Research on the Ecological
Structure of the City

The most distinctive and most widely known development in
the Chicago department in the 1920's was the unprecedented surge of
highly original research in urban ecology. The scholarly output in
these fields was in fact so abundant that the department unintention-
ally and perhaps unwillingly acquired the reputation for almost exclu-
sively concentrating on spatial distributions in its own city. There was
much more to the pattern of departmental activity than this, but the
rapid building of an urban research tradition was an achievement
unique in the history of American sociology. Distant sociologists
tended to classify a scholar as a specialist in human ecology if he were
known to come from the Chicago department, and they often allowed
themselves to suppose that the ecological specialist knew nothing of
other fields of sociology.

Sociological interest in the city originally was influenced from various sources. Because of the rapid growth of cities in the nineteenth
and early twentieth centuries, much popular interest had developed in
the characteristics of the great expanding centers which grew to dominate the cultures of nations. Scholars in history, geography, and other
fields observed and generalized on the almost startling phenomenon of
metropolitan growth, and Charles Booth and others in England pub-

lished abundant descriptions of the new dimensions of misery in urban slum populations. Social surveys and popular descriptive exposés in the United States, especially the writings of Lincoln Steffens, whose *Shame of the Cities* stimulated Robert E. Park, directed further attention to the subject.

Charles Richmond Henderson, an original member of the Chicago department, gave scholarly attention to the city from the start of his sociological career. His interest was perhaps closer to that of the humanitarian than that of the objective scientist, but in the first years of the new university and department he regularly sent graduate students to make observations in various areas of the city. After Henderson's death in 1916, one of his students, Ernest W. Burgess, took over his courses. Thus it was natural for Burgess to establish a large number of working contacts with a variety of community agencies and, although most of these were in the field of social work, their cooperation was to become valuable in the great data-gathering efforts of the urban studies soon to come.

Park early saw the valuable possibilities that lay in using the city of Chicago for research. He urged, verbally and in writing, that the department regard the city as its laboratory.[1] Albion Small favored the proposal, and shortly after the First World War the ecological research activity began to develop.

The first stages of exploration necessarily were mainly descriptive. Mapmaking activity first flourished in Burgess's course in Social Pathology, in which students were sent out to get almost any kind of urban data to make almost any type of map. Indications of urban pattern and structure early became evident, and Burgess and the students perceived that many types of urban phenomena were intercorrelated. Park and Burgess introduced a course in Field Studies to intensify the exploration, and maps of various sociological aspects of Chicago accumulated in the departmental racks and shelves. There were spot maps showing distributions of juvenile delinquents, of criminals of various types, of patrons of dance halls, of movie theaters, of rooming houses, of disorderly houses, and of business and industrial structures of many kinds.[2]

[1] Robert E. Park, "The City: Suggestions for the Investigation of Human Behavior in the Urban Environment," *American Journal of Sociology*, XX (1916), 577–612.

[2] Trial and error plays its part in most rapid developments of graphic devices.

Census tracts for Chicago were first laid out in 1910, and data by tracts were available after each census that followed. The researchers at Chicago added much tract data of their own so that it soon became possible to make use of *rates* of various phenomena in the small subdivisions of the city. The rate maps were far more valuable than spot maps, of course, since the differential density of population gave most spot maps a fairly similar tendency to show a crowding in the central regions of the city.

Mutual respect and cordial personal relations among the members of the social science departments at Chicago led to important cooperation in urban research. The economists and geographers were interested in studies of the city and developed research useful to sociology. Human geography was a major interest of Chicago geographers who studied the physiographic situation of the city and during the 1920's developed within their own discipline the concept of the metropolitan region. This concept was later stated more explicitly and fully by the sociologist R. D. McKenzie. The economists also contributed to the understanding of the city, notably through land-value research covering the entire historical period of Chicago.[3]

Several political scientists conducted research in the urban political system and processes, learning from and contributing to the sociologists' work. Charles Merriam, in fact, participated for a time in city government, serving as Alderman of the Fifth Ward, in which the university was located, and once running unsuccessfully for mayor. Harold Gosnell and C. H. Wooddy contributed research on the connections between urban social disorganization and corruption in city government.[4]

Some of the first spot maps were made by moistening and sticking onto the map little colored glue-backed dots. In addition to making an attractive display, the various colors provided highly visible distinctions which facilitated generalizations. But when a large map marked this way was taken out of a rack and unrolled, a cascade of colored dots broke loose and fell to the floor. Because there was no way of knowing where they had once been pasted, the whole map became worthless. This accident led to the use of ink for the spot maps—more work and less beauty, but they were durable.

[3] Homer Hoyt, *One Hundred Years of Land Values in Chicago* (Chicago: University of Chicago Press, 1933).

[4] Harold F. Gosnell, *Machine Politics: Chicago Model* (Chicago: University of Chicago Press, 1937); and *Negro Politicians* (Chicago: University of Chicago Press, 1935). See also Carroll H. Wooddy, *The Chicago Primary of 1926* (Chicago: University of Chicago Press, 1928).

In the early 1920's a Local Community Research Committee was established which undertook to stimulate interdepartmental studies, concentrating on spatial patterns and forms of cultural life—modes of living, customs, and standards. The first members of this committee were Leon C. Marshall (Head of the Department of Economics), Charles Merriam (Head of Political Science), Edith Abbott (Head of the School of Social Service Administration), Marcus Jernigan (Professor of History), and E. W. Burgess.

The momentum of early urban research in the sociology department and in the whole social science group became an important asset in obtaining additional financial support for research. As the work was proceeding, Beardsley Ruml became the director of the Laura Spelman Rockefeller Foundation, and he induced the trustees to put substantial funds into social science research. In 1923, cooperating social science scholars in various universities established the Social Science Research Council, aided by a grant from the foundation and with prospects of research funds from the same source. The foundation also decided to give direct support to social science research at a number of universities. The first to obtain this kind of direct support was the social science group at the University of Chicago. The result was a great stimulation at the time when it was most appropriate, and interdisciplinary urban research was under way at full speed by the middle of the decade.

Students, including undergraduates, played an important part in the research process. Nearly all sociology courses required term papers, and, while these could be on almost any kind of sociological subject, many involved collection of information on the city. Students made spot maps, rate maps, conducted interviews, attended meetings, and in various ways observed and systematically recorded phenomena of the city. Individually some of these activities may have appeared to be purely descriptive, but they fitted into the growing patterns of urban structure and behavior theory which were developed in lecturing and writing by Park and Burgess, by their colleagues in neighboring departments, and by the more thoughtful graduate students.

A considerable number of graduate dissertations, sometimes built upon term papers, eventually were expanded into books. The major part of the early literature on urban ecology, in fact, is contained in such studies, although the theoretical and summary articles by both Park and Burgess gave direction and unity to the general development. Of particular importance in the latter series are Park's 1916 paper on "The City," mentioned above, and the two symposia, *The City* (1925), edited by both Park and Burgess, and *The Urban Community* (1926), edited by Burgess. Also of significance in this early period was the work by one of Park's first and most creative ecology students, R. D. McKenzie, whose book *The Neighborhood* (Chicago: Unversity of Chicago Press, 1923) was the first in a series of important contributions to human ecology by this author.

In time valuable basic census and social data were accumulated, and it was possible to tabulate this information for each of the subdivisions of Chicago, which were designated *local communities*. Much of the statistical information was originally gathered by census tracts, which numbered about 600 in the 1920's, but they were too small to provide population for stable rates of the various phenomena of interest in sociological research. Combining the census tracts into 75 local communities, however, provided a highly useful device for ecological research. By 1930 a compilation of such information was published in the *Local Community Fact Book of Chicago*, edited by Louis Wirth and Marguerite Furez. This work was reissued after each of the succeeding federal census periods to include the new information as it became available. Some of the more important general research studies in the Chicago studies would not have been possible without this accumulated information.

In their writings and in class lectures by the middle of the 1920's, Park and Burgess had evolved a systematic statement of the character of cities of the same general type as Chicago. A few scholars in other regions of the country who disregarded the explicit qualifications made by Park and Burgess, criticized their formulations by pointing to cities that did not have the characteristic spatial pattern found in Chicago. The Chicago pattern, however, was offered as an example of the general way, apart from local topographical conditions and other special features, by which a modern *urban, industrial, expanding* city takes its form. Cities that developed in other than industrial systems, such as many older cities in Europe, in the Orient, and elsewhere, take an entirely different form. Cities based on vacation resort attractions such as Atlantic City and Miami Beach, would not be expected to take the same shape, nor would governmental cities, shrine cities, educational cities, or various other types.

The ideal-type description of Chicago is of course limited in one other important respect—that of historical era. Because the ecology of cities is not the same in different times, any characterization of the metropolis must always be dated.

With these qualifications, then, a number of useful general statements were made to describe the features of such cities as Chicago. The most fundamental process, perhaps, is that of the cause of the city's growth. Natural increase has not been the main source of population in great American cities; in fact, some cities have had reproduction rates too low even to maintain a population of steady size. The important basis of growth, migration, has had a systematic character. The flows of incoming populations have not spread evenly into the various districts of the city, nor have they expanded the city by adding population on its perimeters in tree-ring growth style. Most of the inflow has been directly into the great central slum districts, which increases the density of already crowded areas.

For the most part, the newly arriving populations were unfamiliar with city life. During the latter decades of the nineteenth century and the early decades of the twentieth century a great flow of European immigrants poured into the central regions of American cities. Some of these immigrants were of urban origins, but most were from rural areas. They were from the lowest income and educational levels of their countries of origin, and in most cases were qualified only for occupations requiring the lowest level of skills. A large proportion necessarily entered factory employment, contributing unskilled labor for low wages. Thus these people could afford only the cheapest residences and so crowded into deteriorating slum tenements.

Part of the new arrivals in the slums occupied dwellings left vacant by earlier populations who had prospered enough to afford moving outward to somewhat more desirable residential areas. Some of the new residents, however, were compressed into houses and apartments in an even higher density, with many families occupying space that formerly housed a single family.

Studies of the residential flow in Chicago revealed a systematic streaming outward from the inner slum zones to the suburbs. Few persons and no ethnic groups made large jumps; the characteristic flow involved a series of small moves, most of which went outward. Each particular ethnic group also tended to disperse steadily over the decades of its average outward movement, and cultural assimilation and some amalgamation by intermarriage accompanied the spatial movement.

In Chicago, as in similar American cities, the flows of new workers came from a succession of sources. The Chicago slums received pulses from German, Irish, Scandanavian, Italian, Polish, and other nationalities, and each of these in turn became dispersed in the outward flow described above. In the early years of the twentieth century the United States was receiving immigrants from peasant areas of Europe at the rate of over a million a year, and most of these settled into the slums of the great industrial cities. After the First World War and the new immigration laws that cut off the larger part of this flow, the city growth did not stop, but the demand for factory labor was then supplied from rural populations of the United States, mainly from the southern regions. Negroes formed a large part of this labor supply, and the Negro populations took their place in the same residential succession. A large proportion of these people came from rural areas, and thus, like the peasants of Europe, were unaccustomed to life in a metropolis.

It is partly a discovery of the Chicago urban research that the characteristic extremes of poverty, disease, and behavior troubles found everywhere in slum populations are products of social disorganization, rather than of low genetic quality in the populations. In the nineteenth century the eugenics movement had persuaded many biological scientists, a considerable number of sociologists, and most of the public that the features of the urban slums were a consequence of generations of selective breeding of defectives—descendants of such families as the Jukes, Kallikaks, and Piney Woods. The evidence was scanty and the research methods hardly worthy of the name, but because of the high prestige of the biological sciences ever since the Darwinian discoveries, the eugenicists' views were widely accepted.

The Chicago research, however, showed that with few exceptions, each racial or national population that poured into the slum areas of the city experienced the same severe disorganization, and that as each of these populations in time prospered and migrated outward into more settled residential districts, the symptoms of disorganization declined. The human behavior pathologies thus were found to be consistently associated with the type of urban area and not with the particular ethnic group which inhabited it. The only exceptions occurred in such populations as had arrived already supplied with some social organization to protect them against the destruction of their old culture—as in the Oriental communities in cities of the west coast and the ghettos populated by European urban Jews already accustomed to problems of city life.

The specific locations of residential areas of various types were found to be influenced by the whole process of competition for favorable urban space. The first choice of desirable pieces of land inevitably is made by the users who can pay the highest prices. The central business district develops at the site most favorable for such enterprises as retail department stores, financial institutions, business and professional offices, headquarters of corporations, dining and entertainment facilities, large transient hotels, and the like. Such agencies as these can extract the most profit from the favored locations and can therefore bid high for the land and pay the high taxes that follow.

The competition for desirable land operates to sort out the agencies and populations in considerable detail. Sociological research in Chicago revealed that this distribution process automatically assigns characteristic locations not only for larger enterprises, but also for a variety of smaller establishments, including music stores, furniture stores, newspaper offices, and physicians' offices of various types.

Outside of the business districts, but bidding for sites as close to them as they can afford, are warehouses, light manufacturing, and other functions that benefit from a central location but require more space than they can buy in the zone of highest land values. Still further out are areas of heavy industry, which could profit from proximity to transportation centers but which need large plots of land.

Residences pay less for land than do business and industry, and so they occupy regions not claimed for commercial use. Thus very few members of the residential population are found near the urban center, except for a few occupants of hotels and some apartment buildings so tall that they are able to make efficient use of the land on which they are based. In general, the residential use of land lies on the far side of the industrial districts. Since the presence of industry makes nearby land unattractive for residential use, the low-income populations crowd into these areas, taking advantage of a local disparity between land values and rental values along the expanding frontier of the industrial area. Residential land lying in the pathway of this expansion rises in potential value in anticipation of eventual favorable sale to industry. The expectation of such sale, however, makes it unprofitable for an owner of a residential building to make permanent improvements or even to keep the building in good repair. For these reasons the rental values in such deteriorating buildings are low enough for the populations with the lowest income. Thus the ecological struggle for space is among the important factors in the location of the slum areas as well as in determining some of their physical features. It must be added that workers with little or no skill also find the industrial slum an appropriate living area because of its proximity to factories in which they work.

Persons with higher incomes seek housing in more attractive areas which are generally further from the central slums of the city so that there is a pattern of direct relationship between amount of wealth and residential distance from the city center. This relationship is made somewhat imperfect, however, by topographical, sentimental, and political features which create desirable living areas that depart from this pattern. In Chicago, for example, the view and fresh breezes along the lake front attract some tall residential building into areas that otherwise might be claimed by light industry. Boston and Philadelphia have areas which were once occupied by slum populations, then later reclaimed for higher-income residences because of the historical sentiment and potential beauty of the older buildings.

Within the broad divisions of the city, sociological research has revealed further details of systematic sorting of populations and functions. Much segregation by ethnic categories, both voluntary and otherwise, exists in the central slums. There are also functional areas with characteristic populations and functions, such as those of the hobo or skid road areas, and the rooming-house districts. These areas are the products of an interaction of forces—such as competition for valuable land, shifts in land use and population flows—which operate in all cities of this type. Such areas do not derive their features merely from a sum of the traits of the people who inhabit them; rather they attract the populations appropriate to their character. Nor are they the results of expressions of the public will through governments, city planners, or community leaders. Hobo and rooming-house areas are strikingly similar in many a large American city, but they were planned that way in none. They are what Park termed *natural areas,* meaning that they are the consequence of natural processes rather than human intentions.

In Park's words: "They are the products of forces that are constantly at work to effect an orderly distribution of populations and functions within the urban complex. They are 'natural' because they are not planned, and because the order that they display is not the result of design, but rather a manifestation of tendencies inherent in the urban situation; tendencies that city plans seek—though not always success-fully—to control and correct. In short, the structure of the city, as we find it, is just as much the product of the struggle and efforts of its people to live and work together collectively as are its local customs, traditions, social ritual, laws, public opinion, and the prevailing moral order." [5]

Early in the period of Chicago urban research Burgess suggested that the major outlines of the city's shape could be represented in a zonal diagram, which in this case was cut nearly in half by the shores of Lake Michigan. In this pattern the central zone was occupied by the business district; the next by a zone in transition, which included the industrial and slum areas and first-settlement areas of many immigrant populations; the third by workingmen's homes outside of the slum; then a residential zone; and finally a commuters' zone. This pattern was later designated the *Burgess zonal hypothesis*, but its purpose was soon gravely misunderstood.

The zonal diagram was never offered as a description of the actual pattern of any city. Burgess spoke of it as an *ideal type*, meaning not that it was the most desirable design for a city, but rather contrasting it with the real in the sense that the drawing of a man in an anatomy textbook is not a description of any actual man, but a representation of the features that are found in most normal men.

A few sociologists who were not fully acquainted with the Park and Burgess contributions developed the misconception that the ecological study of cities implied a neglect of the influence of custom, sentiment, and tradition on patterns of urban growth. In their writings and classroom teachings, however, Park and Burgess consistently empha-sized that a variety of nonecological forces caused departures from the ideal ring pattern and indicated that such special factors were to be found in all cities.

In his opening contribution to the subject, Park was explicit on the influence of culture and subcultural competitive interaction. Through-

[5] Robert E. Park, "Sociology," in Wilson Gee (ed.), *Research in the Social Sciences* (New York: Macmillan, 1929), p. 29.

out his noted 1915 paper on "The City: Suggestions for the Investigation of Human Behavior in the City Environment," [6] statements such as the following occur: "The fact is, however, that the city is rooted in the habits and customs of the people who inhabit it. The consequence is that the city possesses a moral as well as a physical organization, and these two mutually interact in characteristic ways to mold and modify one another. . . . Within the limitations prescribed, however, the inevitable processes of human nature proceed to give these regions and these buildings a character which it is less easy to control."

Thus it is obvious that no pure examples of circular zones were presumed to exist, although ecological research has shown that many cities do conform to the pattern in a general way. For example, an almost universal condition of street design makes circular zones impossible and distorts the zonal boundaries into something like concentric starfish forms. The zonal lines are stretched outward by arterial lines of local transportation—transit systems and major boulevards—and they are further distorted by such topographical features as waterways and hills. In general, heavy industry and business do not find hill sites favorable, while residences do, especially if they provide attractive views, more favorable atmospheric conditions, and separation from noisy traffic.

Other factors allowing exceptions to the zonal pattern are church and educational properties and public lands—parks, boulevards— which are free from the competitive forces that arise from land taxation. These may be out of the natural pattern themselves, and through affecting the attractiveness of adjacent property, may radiate their influence for some distances.

In summary, to the degree that cities are large, industrial, and expanding and are located on flat, featureless land they approximate this zonal pattern, at least in a starfish form. Chicago and Cleveland appear to resemble it most closely; Minneapolis, St. Louis, Milwaukee, and others to an easily perceptible degree. New York and Boston, while not immune to ecological processes, are so influenced by both topography and history that concentric circles seem of little application, and in fact sociologists in those cities have had little tendency to engage in research in human ecology, except to offer them as examples to destroy the Burgess zonal hypothesis.

The significance to sociology of the Chicago ecological research is in

[6] *American Journal of Sociology*, XX, (March, 1915), 577–612, *passim*.

no way dependent on the high visibility of circular zones in the pattern of cities. The important discovery was that a complex ecology does exist, and that it operates in important ways to select populations, to control the direction of their flow, and variously to influence behavior, especially in the variety of manifestations of social disorganization. Since related studies have abundantly shown interconnections of social disorganization and individual behavior difficulties, these ecological systems are clearly an important part of the unified corpus of sociology and to neglect the ecological aspect would leave a gap in the explanation of institutional and individual behavior.

Ecological research has in fact revolutionized sociological understanding of the great slum areas that are found in all great modern cities. As mentioned previously, a half century or more ago all the prestige of science, dominated by biological science, lay behind the explanation of slums in terms of the low biological quality of the populations. The eugenicists had persuaded their colleagues, including many sociologists, of this fact. Poverty, crime, suicide, mental abnormality, and other behavioral defects of slum dwellers were seen as inborn legacies from their defective ancestors who had been reproducing at a higher rate than the normal population. The proposed remedy was a compulsory reversal in the reproduction pattern, involving sterilization of populations of low biological quality and incentives to increase births in populations supposed to be superior. These proposals, which today find little support even among experts in human genetics, were highly respectable earlier in the century and were expressed in legislation for compulsory sterilization in some states considered to be progressive. This doctrine also received important support from Supreme Court Justice Oliver Wendell Holmes in an opinion supporting sterilization legislation which contained the dictum ". . . three generations of imbeciles is enough."

Ecological research has been among the major factors in overthrowing such eugenic extremism. Sociologists have shown that the slum is inhabited by peoples who were not disorganized before migrating to the city. Furthermore, their migration has not been selective of an inferior type of person but has tended more often to select those having somewhat greater ambition and initiative than that possessed by friends and relatives who did not migrate. The various forms of abnormal personal behavior were shown to be a consequence of the experience of social disorganization, more than a cause of it. After a sufficient time each major population that suffered from slum disorganization gradually became adapted to urban life, moved upward in the occupational ladder and outward from the slums, and recovered from the various abnormalities. The personal disorganization was thus a result of a grand and too rapid transition from a pre-industrial folk society to a highly mechanized urban civilization. Few ethnic populations making the transition were able to escape the severe disorganization, but in time all showed the ability to recover from it. This discovery helped to provide a new foundation for sociological comprehension of the whole range of behavior abnormalities, and it opened the gates to what has proved to be the main road of investigation into such phenomena.

Although the fact is not widely acknowledged, a strong connection exists between urban ecological research and the study of socio-economic differentiation which has been in so great vogue in recent years. The schematic zones of the city do describe variations of social class levels almost as well as any other factor, except perhaps for the variable of education. Some scales devised to measure social differentiation in fact employ area of residence as one of the variables. Social climbing involves moving to more favorable residential zones, and social failing may drop a person all the way back to the hobo area of the city. Hence the extensive sociological literature on social differentiation and stratification may be understood as a continuation of one aspect of ecological research along a different dimension.

Urban processes underlie many of the central problems of interest to sociology, and, since our civilization is accelerating in its progress toward complete urbanization, they will probably continue to become of even greater importance in shaping human and social behavior. The nature of cities changes, as does everything in human affairs, and the ecology of cities in 1970 will not be exactly the same as in 1925, but it will not be entirely different either. Concepts and methods for the continuation of this line of interest will evolve along with the other changes.

~⊰ V ⊱~

Urban Behavior Research

The Chicago sociologists never meant that the ecological studies of the city were to be a distinct and separate subject, partitioned off from general sociology. Urban structure was understood as the background of a rich complex of sociological phenomena, and ecology was just one route into the subject. Thomas had written earlier on the problems of social disorganization of Polish peasants transplanted into American cities. Park and Burgess also had prior interests in various questions relating to assimilation and to race relations, and Park had picked up, partly from Simmel, interests in social distance, the characteristics of the stranger, and other phenomena of individuation and isolation. An appreciation also existed for the value of studying specific urban institutions and characteristic natural areas and neighborhoods, all of which were cause and effect of behavior of urban populations. Park regularly sent members of his classes to make small-scale studies of such matters, and Burgess, who did the same thing, also conducted excursions to give his classes a close look at some of the communities and institutions of special sociological interest. Student observations sometimes grew into term papers, term papers into dissertations, and dissertations into books or occasionally a sequence of books. Beginning in the early 1920's, this research interest in a variety of forms of urban behavior resulted in nearly two dozen books in less than two decades.

The first of such studies to reach book form was *The Hobo*, by Nels Anderson. Anderson, who arrived at the university in 1921, had had some experience in hobo life, and his teachers were alert to encourage him to capitalize on his unique firsthand knowledge. They saw an obvious opportunity to connect one of the most characteristic urban districts, the hobo area, with a broader sociological interest in movement, isolation, and disorganization. Burgess had already established a friendship with a Chicago physician, Dr. Ben Reitman, who had an extensive medical practice among the population of the hobo area, as well as human and scientific interests in them. Dr. Reitman joined the sociologists in encouraging Anderson to extend his experience and produce a sociological study, and he was instrumental in obtaining funds to allow Anderson to spend a year living and studying in the Chicago areas of homeless migratory men. The resulting book, *The Hobo* (University of Chicago Press), was published in 1923 as Volume 1 in the *Sociological Series*. Departing from the usual order of degrees and publication, the department allowed Anderson to present the published study as an M.A. thesis. Anderson carried the research no farther, although in 1940 he published *Men on the Move* (University of Chicago Press), in which he gave a quite different treatment of migratory workers in general. In his introduction to this latter book he confessed that in the early study he might have overdramatized the culture of the homeless in Chicago's Hobohemia and that for some years he had been trying to correct this impression.

The Hobo, the first book in the series, was also one of the most colorful. Hobo areas of Chicago were among the least-visited parts of the city, and many readers outside the profession of sociology found the descriptions almost romantically interesting. While ordinary tourists coming to Chicago usually visited parks and museums (and sometimes even the vast stockyards for contrast), it was the University which provided tours for visiting students to such places as Hobohemia, and for a time slumming visits were a fashion among young Chicago intellectuals. Picturesque faces could be seen there in greater variety than in any other part of the city, and the sight of the strange establishments—the employment agencies, the flophouses, the lady barbers, the burlesque shows, the pawnshops—were the next thing in local color to a trip abroad.

The Hobo achieved most of its contribution by way of informal descriptions, using no formal research technique and yielding no new sociological principles. Later works by Anderson, as well as by other students, contained more distinctly sociological value, but as an ice-breaking piece of direct reporting, this project served well. Hoboes, it turned out, were not the easiest persons to study. Some were suspicious or indifferent and would not talk readily to a stranger who was obviously not one of them. Others were gone the next day, or even dead. Walking up to an inhabitant of the hobo area and asking for a life-history interview is a profitless method, and it is little improved by the offer of an inducement to respond.[1]

The Anderson study provided a useful description of the effects of extreme mobility and detachment from society. The most individualistic inhabitant of the hobo area, the bum, is the extreme example of the sociological stranger, and he may be about as incompetent socially as anyone who can be found outside an institution such as a prison or mental hospital. In contrast to him the hobo or migratory worker, who often temporarily occupies the same urban area as the bum, takes part in cooperative structures and experiences less personality deterioration.

Anderson's contribution was augmented by two later studies. Harvey Zorbaugh, whose book is discussed later in this chapter, included a picturesque and somewhat journalistic description of one of the hobo areas on the near north side of Chicago, the North Clark Street hobohemia. This area was similar to the other two hobo areas in Chicago in most respects, but it had one feature lacking in the others—a tradition of intellectual and political street discussion somewhat similar to that of Hyde Park in London. It was also ecologically interesting because of its proximity to the Gold Coast, the strip of fashionable and expensive apartment buildings and hotels on the lake front.

[1] A few years after *The Hobo* was published, another graduate student at Chicago undertook to gather a series of hobo life histories. He arranged an affiliation with a church mission which maintained a rescue station in the hobo area. The mission invited homeless men from the street to come in for religious services and refreshments, but the men had to be "saved" before they were fed. After a dinner, the rescued men were to be given a bed for the night, breakfast in the morning, and help in finding a job during the next two or three days. The student planned to start his life-history interviews at the end of the hobo's first day of job hunting. This research effort was a complete failure; no hobo ever came back for a second night, and no life histories were obtained.

Some years later a further study of men of the hobo area was conducted by Edwin H. Sutherland and Harvey J. Locke and published in 1936 under the title *10,000 Homeless Men*. Again the results were essentially consistent with the characteristics described in the Anderson study. Among the details of interest in the Sutherland and Locke study is a discussion of skilled adaptation to poverty by some of the homeless men, including successful techniques of street begging.

Although names vary—"Main Stem," "Skid Road" (sometimes through misunderstanding "Skid Row"), "The Bowery"—the phenomenon of the hobo area is found in most large cities and tends to be similar in all of them. Such areas have characteristic locations near the central business district, and many distinctive institutions, such as cheap hotels or flophouses, pawnshops, burlesque theaters, barber colleges, and the like. The population fluctuates according to the season of the year and the prosperity of the times, but it is composed principally of men who are migratory workers, migratory nonworkers, and nonmigratory nonworkers. Various indices of disorganization are higher here than in any other typical area of the city. The week-end police-court haul of drunks is greatest from this area, and the rate of chronic alcoholism is always high. Death rates, especially from tuberculosis and venereal disease, are high, and the rates of hospitalization for mental disorders are the highest, or among the highest, in the metropolitan area. The area is at least in part a product of the natural forces mentioned by Park, being an ecological and sociological entity not planned or wanted by anyone but occurring in a remarkably uniform shape in city after city and persisting in the face of public aversion and official disapproval. For the most part, such actions as zoning and city planning have not affected it.

A contrasting line of urban research is found in the studies of family disorganization. In spite of the fact that he never married, E. W. Burgess became the department authority on the sociology of the family, and during his whole career devoted a major part of his research energy to the subject. Some of the research concerned aspects of the family other than ecological, but one of his earlier students, Ernest R. Mowrer, gave attention to variations in family behavior in the different parts of the city. The first results of Mowrer's study appeared in his doctoral dissertation of 1924, amplified and published as *Family Disorganization* in 1927.

On the basis of his ecological research, Mowrer divided Chicago into five area types with reference to the character of the family. These were designated as:

1. *Nonfamily areas,* principally the hobo districts, populated by males, most of them unmarried and the rest separated from their wives.
2. *Emancipated family areas,* consisting of rooming-house, hotel, and apartment-hotel districts, "Where conventional roles between husbands and wives give way to individualism," and where few marriages involve children.
3. *Paternal family areas,* inhabited by immigrant populations and others of low income and education in which the tradition of the dominant father prevails.
4. *Equalitarian family areas,* in which the traditional middle-income style of unified family is found.
5. *Maternal family areas,* characteristic of commuter suburbs, involving an income–earning father absent from the household weekdays and sometimes until midevening, so that the wife is required to carry many of the duties of the head of a household.

Mowrer placed these areas into the same concentric circle scheme proposed by Burgess, but he also recognized that this presentation was a simplification of the actual distributions. Although such circles are admittedly not visible in all cities, these five broad divisions of family types exist in every large American metropolis. Thus the competitive forces which Park found to produce the general structure of urban areas also impose important characteristics on the ancient and venerable institution of the family.

Such broad connections of ecology and family types do not complete the account of Mowrer's research in this field. Perhaps the most important effect of the city on family life lies in the connections between the intense social disorganization in certain urban areas and the disorganization of family life. The research effort thus led logically into inquiry into the processes of family failures. Under the title of *Domestic Discord,* published in 1928, Mowrer and his wife Harriet R. Mowrer continued this direction of investigation, which both have maintained over the many years of their productive careers.

Phenomena of race had been of interest to sociologists and anthropologists in the nineteenth century, but an important part of their interest was expressed in a comparison of racial mental capacities and a related eugenics concern. Cooley was among the early sociologists to question the then widely held views of racial inequality, and in 1918 Faris published a challenge to some of the popular reasoning on the topic, drawing from his earlier experiences with natives of the Congo.[2] Park, as mentioned before, applied himself to the particular experiences of the Negro race in both Africa and America and provided important stimulation to general sociological interest in race relations.

The concern with issues of Negro-white interaction at Chicago was increased by the 1919 race riot in that city, which lasted nearly a week and cost the lives of 38 persons, the injury of 537 others, and the loss of housing for about a thousand persons. The riot was studied by Graham R. Taylor, in collaboration with Charles S. Johnson and others.[3] The resulting book contributed further to sociological interest in relationships of race, collective behavior, and social disorganization.

During the 1920's, E. Franklin Frazier initiated a series of investigations on the sociology of the Negro family. In his first book, *The Negro Family in Chicago,* which was developed from his dissertation and published in 1932, Frazier established some systematic relations of the Negro family experience to the ecological zones of Chicago; in *The Negro Family in the United States,* published in 1939, he attempted to do the same thing for other cities. The Negro districts at that time extended for the most part through the series of urban zones so that some of the Negro population was found in each. In the Harlem Negro community of New York city, for example, the marriage rate was found to vary systematically by such zones; for males the percentages then married in 1930 from the innermost Zone I outward were shown to be, respectively, 50, 56, 60, 62, and 64. For females the percentages were: 51, 55, 58, 60, and 60. Rates of home ownership, long regarded as a useful index of family stability, varied even more. Using the same types of zones in the District of Columbia in 1940 the range was 3, 9, 17, 28, and 51.

Similar statistical data in the Frazier research indicated significant

[2] Charles H. Cooley, "Genius, Fame and the Comparison of Races," *Annals of the American Academy of Political and Social Science,* Vol. LX, No. 3 (May, 1897); and Ellsworth Faris, "The Mental Capacity of Savages," *American Journal of Sociology,* XXIII (1918), 603–619.

[3] Chicago Commission on Race Relations, *The Negro in Chicago* (Chicago: University of Chicago Press, 1922).

zonal variation of age of women, number of children under five years old, and births. In Harlem in 1930 births were found to increase from 66 (per 1,000 married women) in Zone I to 168 in Zone V.

One of the striking aspects of large industrial cities in the United States is the presence of highly segregated communities of various immigrant populations. As stated in a previous chapter, the main source of growth of the industrial cities until the First World War was the successive waves of immigrant populations from the agricultural regions of Europe. Most cities had a Germantown, a Little Italy, a Polish district, and various other nationality settlements. Some of these, such as the Chinatowns, were colorful enough to become tourist attractions. All of them were of interest to the sociologist, and a practice soon developed at Chicago, as elsewhere, of arranging class visits to such communities. Term papers and dissertations naturally followed, and in time, research volumes.

The Jewish communities were of special interest, partly because of their differences from most of the other ethnic districts. An important part of their members came from the larger cities of Europe and thus did not have to experience the transition from peasant to city life which other nationalities found so disorganizing. In their centuries of experience in European ghettos the Jews had evolved customs and institutions to protect themselves and their cultural heritage from the destructive influences of the surrounding societies, and some of these protective devices were transplanted to their communities in the cities of the United States.

Louis Wirth, whose 1925 doctoral dissertation had been on the same subject, published *The Ghetto* in 1928 and related the Chicago experience of the immigrant Jews to the ecology of the city and to their past experiences in the European ghettos. Wirth considered the ghetto to be of sociological interest for several reasons. For one thing, it represents a phenomenon of prolonged isolation of a people, permitting the preservation of a distinct culture in the face of urban conditions which would ordinarily produce rapid assimilation. He also saw the ghetto as a form of accommodation through which a minority is subordinated to a dominant group, while at the same time experiencing a degree of toleration in the face of contrasts that are potential sources of conflict.

The European ghettos, with a five-hundred-year history, eventually evolved into a stable form. While having some of the same characteristics and serving some of the same functions as their European counterparts, the first-settlement Jewish communities in cities of the United States have more of a transitional character. In the latter communities there has been a stream of migration away from the ghetto, going through second-settlement Jewish areas and afterward scattering into the general population and undergoing assimilation.

Wirth's interests were less in the Jewish ghetto as such than in what Park called the natural history of such settlements. His study thus was meant to enrich sociological knowledge of such non-Jewish settlements as Little Sicilies, Chinatowns, Negro districts, and other ethnic areas of the city, and to some extent Bohemias and Hobohemias and other specialized communities. The feature of the ghetto Wirth emphasized most, however, was its capacity to act corporately. He wrote of it as not merely an ecological phenomenon, not merely a physical fact, but also as a state of mind.

Under the stimulation of Park, Pauline V. Young undertook a study similar in general direction to those of Wirth. She investigated the experience of a self-segregated religious cult in Los Angeles, the Molokans, and published it in 1932 under the title *Pilgrims of Russian Town*. Although her approach was essentially descriptive, it involved what came to be called *participant observation*, which meant taking some part in the lives of the members of the community while preserving enough personal detachment to avoid losing objectivity. Park had specifically advised her to "think and feel Molokan" in order to gain a complete understanding of the Molokan culture, social world, and inner life, but at the same time to avoid forming an emotional attachment which would inject a fatal bias into her findings. Presumably she did her best, although a ring of affection for and admiration of her subjects seems to radiate from her descriptions of them.

The essential finding of the Molokan research was again that a separate culture can be defended against disorganization in a modern city, provided that sufficient isolation can be preserved. The Molokans held as far as possible to their own language, to their own customs and manner of dress, to a strong emphasis on their religion, and to a requirement of being together as much of the time as the necessities of making a living permitted.

Carl A. Dawson, another student and admirer of Park, extended ethnic research through his own investigations and those of his McGill

University students to a number of Canadian ethnic groups, including the Doukhobors, the Mennonites, the Mormons, the German-Catholics, and the French-Canadians in *Group Settlement: Ethnic Communities in Western Canada* (1936). Everett C. Hughes, also a Park protégé, later made important contributions to the French-Canadian investigations through various articles as well as the book *French Canada in Transition*, published in 1943.

Perhaps the most conspicuous aspect of the reputation of the city of Chicago in the 1920's was the magnitude of its crime. Beer wars, bombings, racketeering, holdups, and gang murders made newspaper copy all over the world. One of the most famous citizens of Chicago in this period was Al Capone, boss of the underworld, who achieved such renown that some prominent noncriminal visitors to the city even sought introductions. The interrelations of organized crime and city politics were so strong that corruption sometimes reached into the city administration and the police system.

Lincoln Steffens, in his widely read journalistic account *The Shame of the Cities* (1904), had surveyed essentially the same conditions in a number of large cities and had sought a general explanation of the phenomena of organized crime and corruption. Steffens, however, possessed no method other than his own observations and reasoning ability and consequently could not be expected to produce a set of scientific findings through his sole efforts.

Park, an admirer of Steffens's writings on the subject, and his colleague Burgess, along with many other scholars and students, perceived that here was a rich opportunity for research into the causes of crime. Their work was effected mainly through their students, both undergraduate and graduate, and stimulated information-gathering expeditions, term papers, dissertations, and books.

Since it was apparent that most patterns of criminal behavior are acquired during the criminal's youthful days, research into the origins of juvenile delinquency appeared to be of strategic importance. Burgess's undergraduate students early systematically surveyed opinions of persons then responsible for dealing with the problem in Chicago— policemen, judges, probation officers, and social workers. Students from sociology classes interviewed these officials and tabulated their responses, but they could find no clear or useful knowledge of causes.

The most common explanation of delinquency offered by probation officers, for example, was simply "poverty." Many social workers were still dominated by the declining eugenics viewpoint which considered the delinquent to be an atavistic form of biological inferior. Others were attracted to medical theories and psychiatric insights which appeared too individualistic to appeal to the sociologist, especially in the absence of a satisfactory method apart from the intuition of the expert.

Other writers, including even such psychiatric authors as William Healy in Boston, had perceived the strong tendency for urban juvenile delinquency to occur in groups of boys rather than by solitary individuals. Study of boy gangs thus appeared to be a promising point of entry into criminological research, and some literature on the subject already existed when Frederic Thrasher began his study of boy gangs in Chicago. In 1918 he had already presented a master's thesis on the Boy Scouts, an organization which then and for many years to come made implausible claims to preventing delinquency. This study was followed by intensive, direct participation in activities with boy gangs, including delinquent gangs, in Chicago. He counted such gangs in the city and produced the interesting total of 1,313, a number which undergraduates in sociology classes for the next twenty years found easy to remember.

Thrasher observed that the gangs were especially prevalent in the *interstitial zones* of the city—the great central slums already known to be the breeding ground for most professional crime. His interpretation of the behavior of the boys, however, was far more sociological than the theories of medical men and correctional officials mentioned above. Thrasher found the boys to be psychologically normal, and the phenomenon of gang formation a natural sociological development. In the abstract of his 1936 thesis he stated: "The gang is an interstitial group originally formed spontaneously, and then integrated through conflict. It is characterized by the following types of behavior: meeting face to face, milling, movement through space as a unit, conflict, and planning. The result of this collective behavior is the development of tradition, unreflective internal structure, esprit de corps, solidarity, morale, group awareness, and attachment to a local territory."

The motivation of the gang behavior, far from being caused by psychological abnormality, appeared to be based on normal sociability and an appetite for excitement and adventure. Not all of the boy gangs' activities were criminal, but Thrasher found the community forces that curb illegal behavior were weak or inoperative in these areas of the city. He observed that ". . . the gang in Chicago is primarily a phenomenon of the children of foreign-born immigrants. The child of the immigrants tends to escape parental control and become superficially Americanized. The normally directing institutions of family, school, church, and recreation break down on the intramural frontier of gangland and the gang arises as a sort of substitute organization." Thrasher further stated that the gangs encouraged truancy in their members, and because they taught forms of delinquency which ultimately led into criminality, they were an important factor in the support of organized crime.

In the same period as Thrasher's work, Clifford R. Shaw and his associates, operating from the Illinois Institute for Juvenile Research cooperating closely with Burgess and graduate students at Chicago, were gaining momentum in their long and productive research in juvenile delinquency. One of the first steps in this investigation was to check on earlier and current concepts of delinquency causation. A highly popular belief among social workers in the 1920's, for example, was that broken homes were important in causing delinquency. Uncriticized statistical information seemed to support this idea, since a higher proportion of delinquents than nondelinquents lived in incomplete families. An observation in New York City, for example, indicated that the ratio of juvenile delinquents from broken homes proportional to those from unbroken homes was 1.5 to 1.[4] These were uncontrolled data, however. Shaw and McKay made a more careful study in Chicago, matching the delinquents and nondelinquents for age and nationality, and found a ratio of only 1.18 to 1.[5] Subsequent research has supported this latter finding.

Shaw and McKay also undertook a full test of the observation that most delinquency originates in the disorganized areas of the city and produced extensive research on this point, not only from Chicago, but also from Philadelphia, Cleveland, Birmingham, Denver, Seattle, and

[4] John Slawson, *The Delinquent Boy* (Boston: R. C. Badger, 1926), pp. 354–365.
[5] Clifford R. Shaw and Henry D. McKay, *Social Factors in Juvenile Delinquency* (Washington, D.C.: U.S. Printing Office, 1931), pp. 273–284.

Richmond. In view of their thoroughness, the findings are difficult to dispute. From whatever source the figures were drawn and for as many decades back as data for Chicago were available, the rates of delinquent behavior were highest in the central slum areas and successively lower in each of the urban zones outward to the suburbs. In general, the high rate for the central zones persisted through successive occupation by different ethnic groups, and, as stated in an earlier chapter, the specific rate for each ethnic group declined as its members moved to other zones.

There has been some disposition, especially by those other than sociologists, to explain this finding by the contention that it is an artificial result of inaccurate information. For example, some have argued that boys are delinquent in all parts of a city but that in the high-income areas the parents are better able to keep their children out of the hands and the records of the police. Questionnaire studies asking boys if they ever performed any of a list of infractions have shown that most boys from any kind of social background have at some time performed actions that could be classified as delinquent. But the more serious crimes that tend to lead to adult criminality—such as shoplifting, burglary, robbery, and car theft—were in fact extremely rare among boys living in the outlying high-income suburbs of Chicago and extremely common in the areas of highest delinquency rates. In the Shaw research, many types of evidence converge on this conclusion, including the area variation in rates of truancy from public schools, which is less subject to protection by powerful parents.

A second important phase of the research consisted of the life-history studies of the development of the delinquent pattern in the individual boy. The investigators at the Institute for Juvenile Research and graduate students at the University of Chicago gathered such cases by the thousands. Shaw's customary procedure in getting a life history was to persuade a boy in a correctional institution to write it for him by convincing him that no authorities would have the information and promising him that it would be used for research purposes only. In a typical case a boy would first write only a brief account of his whole life. Shaw would then have it expanded by pointing to a particular section, remarking that it interested him, and asking for more details on that part. This procedure was repeated for other sections, and sometimes for parts within an expanded section. Three of these life histories were even enlarged to book length.[6] More recently Burgess has written of the value of Shaw's life-history studies as follows: "Because of the daily contacts . . . with a wide variety of delinquents and with judges, probation officers, court social workers, and civic leaders throughout the community, his research was able to bring a realism to criminology and especially the study of juvenile delinquency which had been conspicuously scarce in American sociology before 1920. In fact, empirical American sociology was perhaps popularized and transmitted to all corners of the world by the Shaw monographs more than by any other examples of this brand of social research."[7]

Shaw's generalizations should be limited to the type of juvenile delinquent found in the highly disorganized urban slums, but for this type he was able to provide strong support for the general conclusion that psychological abnormality in the individual was not an important causal factor. The motivation in each boy for beginning and continuing delinquent behavior was found to be normal and social. In fact, after some years and many hundreds of case studies, Shaw was able to state in lectures to graduate students at Chicago that he had not yet found a boy who had committed his first delinquent act alone. In every case the boy was led into delinquency by other experienced delinquents, and his motivation was mainly to conform to the expectations of a primary group. There was no indication of neurosis, of frustrated aspiration, or of rebelliousness against parents in the accounts of this behavior, nor for that matter of the hunger drive that is based on poverty. A most common form of first delinquency was found to be something like a group raid on a fruit stand before a grocery store. The boys would snatch handfuls of fruit and run, and if chased by the proprietor, discard some of the loot at his feet in order to be amused by his indecision whether to retrieve his property or continue the chase. Some of the fruit might be eaten, but most of it was

[6] *The Jack-Roller: A Delinquent Boy's Own Story* (Chicago: University of Chicago Press, 1930); *The Natural History of a Delinquent Career* (Chicago: University of Chicago Press, 1931); *Brothers in Crime* (Chicago: University of Chicago Press, 1938).

[7] Ernest W. Burgess and Donald J. Bogue, *Contributions to Urban Sociology* (Chicago: University of Chicago Press, 1964), p. 591.

discarded. The boys often wrote that the excitement was the principal reward for this activity.

Not only the initial delinquent action for each boy, but most of his subsequent delinquent behavior was committed in groups or small gangs. The group perpetuated techniques of various types of theft and avoidance of detection and punishment and motivated the boys to graduate to more advanced, difficult, and financially rewarding types of crime as they grew older. All of this development was possible in the slum areas because of the disorganization of the community and the political processes that operate to control behavior in more stable neighborhoods.

Burgess has warned, however, against a more recent viewpoint held by some sociologists that overestimates the breach between the delinquent culture and the adult society: "Some, especially those who had comparatively little firsthand research contact with the delinquency world, came to view the delinquency subculture as a whole and complete social system in itself—a self-sustaining society at war with established society—a more or less autonomous social entity and reality. Shaw and McKay did not take this extreme a view, and regarded this as a somewhat mischievous overstatement of the delinquency reality that exists. In their view, the delinquency tradition exists in constant interaction with the larger culture of the community and the neighborhood, and bears the unmistakable stamp of that culture. For example, the status of boys in the gang is found not to be independent of the status of their parents in the neighborhood . . ." [8]

Having found that the burden of a massive amount of research evidence pointed toward general neighborhood disorganization among the basic causes of delinquent behavior, Shaw and his associates attempted to test the hypotheses by making extensive measures to rebuild organization in a community with a high delinquency rate. This effort, originally known as the Chicago Area Project, has been carried on for more than two decades, but the difficulties of satisfactorily evaluating the results leave unresolved the issue of success in reducing delinquency.

While the Shaw group was conducting its early studies of juvenile crime in the 1920's, other research was undertaken on the larger forms

[8] Burgess and Bogue, *op. cit.,* p. 598.

of adult criminality and their connections with political corruption. E. H. Sutherland studied the ways of the professional criminal and later the phenomenon he termed white-collar criminality, meanwhile developing his general theoretical statement of the principal of differential association as the basic cause of all criminal behavior.[9]

At the same time, John Landesco, a graduate student, undertook a general description of the adult criminal organization in Chicago. Supported by a research grant, he devoted full time to this investigation for more than a year. With the advantage of years of residence in disorganized Chicago districts and personal acquaintance with a variety of inhabitants, Landesco was well equipped to gain the confidence of the persons he was studying and could speak with ease in their manner. He established useful contacts with a number of gangsters, some of whom later made newspaper headlines as victims of gang warfare. Because he always made his research purpose clear and promised to treat information confidentially, he was able to go directly from gangster to policeman with both sides knowing this fact and neither attempting to persuade him to give useful information about the other.

The principal published result of the Landesco research is descriptive in an essentially journalistic style.[10] Although lacking in method, it gave a useful general picture of the size, penetration, and cost to society of the intricate alliance of the underworld and the political machine. Landesco considered that he had made a strong case for conclusions such as the following:

1. The underworld organization of Chicago, containing interlocking activities in commercialized vice, gambling, bootlegging, and gang crimes and enforcing its decrees by bombs, murder, and other violent and illegal methods, had a long continuity in the history of the city.
2. The extralegal government had no formal organization but was held together in a kind of feudal system by powerful leaders, personal loyalties, alliances and agreements, and even a code of morals.

[9] Edwin H. Sutherland, *The Professional Thief* (Chicago: University of Chicago Press, 1937); and "White-Collar Criminality," *American Sociological Review,* V (February, 1940), 1–12.
[10] John Landesco, *Organized Crime in Chicago,* Part III of The Illinois Crime Survey (Chicago: Illinois Association for Criminal Justice, 1929).

3. The continuity of the leadership in the criminal underworld, which had only three overlords in a twenty-five-year period, was greatly superior to that of the police organization, which had thirteen chiefs in the same period and only one of these served a full term.

4. Criminal enterprise spread into fields ordinarily controlled by other interests, such as liquor distribution and labor unions.

5. Friendships and other informal alliances between gangsters and politicians operated to give almost complete immunity from detection and prosecution to high officials in the underworld organization.

Landesco also perceived the relation between the delinquent boy gangs and the elaborate structure of organized adult crime. The basic conditions of social disorganization in the city appeared to constitute the fundamental cause of the whole phenomenon of chronic professional criminality, and to the extent that this is true it would account for the resistance of crime to all varieties of prevention and treatment efforts directed toward changing the behavior of the individual criminal. The few attempts to alter the organized social environment of juvenile delinquents have also reported very little success, since most of the efforts are directed toward only a small segment of the boy's social world. It may thus be conjectured that the only pathway to the elimination or major reduction of professional crime may require the reestablishment in urban slums of the sort of social organization that holds misdeeds to a manageable level in the more settled residential and suburban communities.

A part of the color of any large city, and to some extent the basis of its appeal to visitors, is its various types of people and standards of behavior. One consequence of the mobility of urban populations is the emancipation it provides for persons who seek it. In general, the more mobile the population of an area, the greater is the rate of unconventional behavior. W. I. Thomas appeared to view the great city as a place where not only the bohemian character type but also the creative nonconformist could flourish. Although less concerned than Thomas with personal freedom, Park also was fascinated with the many ways in which the sociological stranger in the city uses his freedom from the conventional social control of the village.

Park encouraged some of his students to select aspects of urban life in which such freedom and sometimes personal disorganization is found and to carry this interest into a series of term papers, a thesis or two, and in some cases a book. The experience of Norman S. Hayner is representative of this process. Having completed an M.A. thesis in 1921 under the direction of Burgess, Hayner turned his interests toward those of Park and began to enroll in Park's courses and seminars. In a 1921 summer course, The Social Survey, he heard Park talk at length on matters relating to mobility and the stranger. After a month in the course, Hayner had a long interview with Park and recorded in his diary that it dealt with such matters as "traveling men, elevator men, janitors, bartenders, newsboys, waitresses, stenographers, young business women, shop girls, sweatshop workers."

The next day at a meeting called for students interested in community studies, Park again talked at length. A committee was organized for such studies, with an executive committee composed of Park himself, Erle Fisk Young, R. D. McKenzie, Carl A. Dawson, Dwight Sanderson, and a secretary, Augustus F. Kuhlman. Many of the group later produced well-known publications in this field.

For his course project with Park, Hayner decided to work on maps of clubs, saloons, and cafes in the loop district of Chicago, and for another course he made a study of a disintegrated neighborhood. Late in the quarter he had a talk lasting an hour and a half with Park and received further inspiration for his research. In October he held a conference with Park about a possible thesis and began to focus on hotels, having in mind a study of the Loop District as a type of hotel business center. Another interview with Park occurred three days later on October 10. At a meeting of the Society for Social Research on October 13, 1921, Park presented to the audience a general plan for the study of Chicago, and, according to Hayner, "secured the endorsement of the society."

The following morning Hayner had still another interview with Park and formulated as a thesis topic "The Hotel Population of Chicago: An Aspect of the Housing Problem." In his diary entry for that date Hayner asks, "Is a hotel a home? What is mobility?" In his seminar with Ellsworth Faris the same quarter Hayner chose to study "Mobility of the City Population" and started to make a map of the hotels in Chicago. On October 26 he interviewed Park again about hotels, and Park expressed a strong interest in the proposed map of the Loop hotels and promised to take a trip there with Hayner and "nose around." On November 1 Hayner started exploring hotels in the Loop, noting the ground area covered, heights of buildings, location of entrances, and other general characteristics. The next day he spent three more hours doing the same.

On November 8 and 11 he talked with Faris and recorded in his notes "Helpful suggestions for the study of mobility" of the first meeting, and "Began with mobility and ended with religion" for the second. The notes also mention a seminar discussion of Hayner's use of the term "mobility" and report the consensus that his definition was so broad as to make the term valueless.

Late in November Hayner had a meeting with Park, Burgess, and a Mrs. Donovan, who was acquainted with persons in some of the leading hotels of Chicago and promised to help distribute a questionnaire if Hayner would devise one. On December 1 he reports finding good materials on hotels in the public library. A week later he obtained another interview with Park and planned to take a course in Field Studies with Park and Burgess, and a course in Social Forces, and to work on his hotel studies in both. He did not wait for the winter quarter to begin work, however, and records for December 17 that he "hiked about seven or eight miles through drizzling rain, wind, and later snow and gale checking up map of hotels in Woodlawn and Hyde Park." Three days later he did a similar checkup for the Wilson District. On January 6 the promised exploration of the Loop with Park took place, which lasted from 9 a.m. to 5:30 that afternoon and included visits to a real-estate office, the Chicago Real Estate Board, and the Public Library. Hayner also notes, "Over lunch Park told his life story."

For his projects in his three winter-quarter courses, Hayner decided to undertake the following projects: "Leisure of Women in Hotels," "Classification of Hotels on the Basis of Size and Mobility of Population," and "Outlying Centers of Mobility like 63rd Street and Cottage Grove Avenue."

In the seminar Park spent practically all the time discussing the logical problem in defining a hotel and the significance of mobility. On January 10 Hayner records hearing Park read "an exceedingly interesting paper on Hobohemia in the class on Social Forces." Two days after this entry, Hayner records that he presented a report in one of his classes, "Hotel Population of Chicago: An Aspect of the Housing Problem," and received many questions from the class.

During the latter half of January Hayner made six visits to hotels or hotel areas, such as the 63rd and Cottage Grove area, where he "noted crowds, lights, theaters, parked cars, hotels, restaurants, banks, etc." He also worked out questions for a census of hotel population, but two days afterward he recorded that Park did not think much of the census method, especially if the questionnaires were to be sent by mail. On January 24th, Hayner personally took a census of the Washington Park Hotel and entered "a very promising beginning."

In mid-February Hayner notes a report he presented to the class on Social Forces, and records, "Did not have my material well enough organized"; but at the end of the month after a report to Park's seminar, the latter said, "That's very good, Mr. Hayner. You are certainly working that out." Park went on to suggest a study of the habits centering about the home, the apartment, and the hotel.

The actual thesis work began in early April, and the excursions in search of data, as well as the interviews with Park, continued. Hayner also interviewed Albion Small about the latter's hotel experiences.

On May 23, Park suggested to Hayner that he begin writing, and in another ninety-minute interview, approved the outline. By June 21 he reports completion of the first draft of the introductory chapter, "The Hotel as an Index of Urban Life," while continuing to gather material. An entry of June 22 reports a visit to a hotel in a hobo district to interview Nels Anderson. They talked for nearly an hour, and Hayner was, as he said, "shown the sights." A week later Park spoke of the draft of the introductory chapter as very good and said that if Hayner could work out the rest of the thesis that way he would have something at the end of the summer. The writing continued, and so did the gathering of material. Hayner notes that he attended a musical comedy, "The Hotel House," on August 5.

The completed thesis, accepted in 1923, pleased Park and he encouraged Hayner to publish it as a book. *Hotel Life* finally appeared in 1936, many years after the principal investigation was conducted. It gave flesh to the speculations of Simmel and the imaginative thoughts of Park on the various consequences of mobility and detachment on behavior.

Park did not scorn research methods and spoke of the desirability of developing improved techniques of discovery, but he also considered as very valuable the informal gathering and organization of material in the fashion of the thoughtful journalist. It was under his influence that Harvey Zorbaugh brought out a study that was a best seller in Chicago —*The Gold Coast and the Slum*, published in 1929. The book is a rich and interesting description of an area of the near north side, in which a strip of expensive hotels and apartment hotels along the lake front stood adjacent to a narrow area of rooming houses, and just beyond that, one of the severely disorganized slums of the city. Although little permanent contribution to human ecology or social disorganization resulted from this study, it did follow Park's general approach by attempting to find the natural processes which determine the characteristics of the picturesque urban areas. The wide circulation of the book may also have aided sociology by stimulating public interest and understanding of urban studies at the university.

A study closely related to the research on delinquency and crime was the investigation made by Walter C. Reckless into the nature of organized commercialized prostitution. This research was conducted during the 1920's and was published as *Vice in Chicago* in 1933.

In the period of this study commercialized vice grew out of the same complex of disorganization that supported the high crime rates in Chicago. When the alliance between organized crime and corrupt political administrations was most stable, the commercial vice in the city operated as one of the large business enterprises, along with liquor distribution, rackets, and organized gambling. In such periods the vice resorts operated almost openly, with little interference from police or other officials. They were generally located in districts suitable to their special requirements and convenient to the population which furnished the most patronage. The rooming-house districts thus were the areas most favorable for commercial vice because the high rate of population mobility helped to furnish anonymity and reduced the power of the neighborhood to interfere with the operation of houses of prostitution.

Among the significant findings of the Reckless study was confirmation of the high rate of patronage of prostitution resorts by men from the hobo and rooming-house districts. Maps showing the distribution

of residences of men arrested in vice raids revealed a high concentration in these districts, as did maps showing the incidence of venereal
disease and deaths attributed to this disease.

In periods of reform which from time to time swept the corrupt
officials out of office, the stable alliance of police and commercial vice
was sometimes interrupted so that the resorts could no longer operate
openly. Some houses retreated to smaller, more furtive establishments,
and others found industrial suburbs with sufficient disorganization to
be hospitable to their undertakings. Because these suburban vice
establishments favored proximity to the city, some located close to the
city limits, and one even occupied a house that straddled the city and
state boundary so that in case of a sudden raid the occupants needed
only to move to the other end of the building to escape arrest.

Another phenomenon of the same areas answering to a similar
desire is the taxi-dance hall—the dance establishment which furnishes
female dancing partners for a fee to men who come alone. These halls
were not illegal and served a population somewhat similar to that
supporting vice resorts—the nonfamily men of the mobile rooming-
house areas and the strangers passing through the city. The taxi-dance
halls were usually located at major transportation intersections in the
rooming-house districts and were a minor part of the complex of
institutions of those areas responding to the isolation and loneliness
common in their inhabitants.

One of the more important studies of disorganization in the 1920's
was *Suicide*, published in 1928 by Ruth S. Cavan. This book, which
grew out of a series of term papers and a thesis, was written during the
years the author supported herself by working as department secretary.

The Cavan study had a fundamental relationship to the Park and
Burgess teachings on urban ecology. One of its basic findings was that
the incidence of suicide in Chicago was greatest in the highly disorganized central hobo and rooming-house areas of the city and lowest
in the most stable residential areas. The highest rate of all occurred in
the Loop, with the next highest rates in areas contiguous to it. Inspec-
tion of the figures by sex, however, indicated that this concentration
was mainly one of male suicides. Few women inhabit these central
hobo areas, and the few who do are not in a life situation comparable
to that of the homeless migratory male.

These observations comport with suicide research in the tradition extending through Durkheim and his student Maurice Halbwachs into present-day ecological and statistical studies. Other studies conducted by sociologists in a number of cities have supported the basic connection between conditions of social disorganization and suicide in western civilization. Satisfied of the fact of such a connection, Cavan turned her attention to the process in the individual that leads to suicide, obtaining information through cases and life-history studies.

The three principal factors in individual suicide appeared to be some sort of crisis, weak social controls operating against suicide, and a personality factor that contributes toward the choice of self-destruction in a crisis. A common type of crisis seems to grow out of events which shatter the life-organization of a person. If a career or a marriage or any specific major goal is the core of all the organized aspirations of a person, its destruction may weaken or destroy his motivation to live. This fact alone does not seem to be sufficient to cause suicide; many persons live on because of obligations to family, friends, and the community. Mobile and detached persons or residents of disorganized areas, however, are partly or entirely free of social pressure to continue to live when life is burdensome. The personality factor, which is less defined, may differentiate the kind of man who gives up and ends his life in case of failure, rather than making a fresh start, perhaps by moving to another area and rebuilding his life on a new base. In case studies, Cavan found some indications that a pattern of giving up in a crisis may develop early in childhood and may even have a relation to the wish expressed by a few children never to have been born.

Similar in spirit to the Cavan research, and growing out of inspiration from the same teachers and fellow students, was the volume by Robert E. L. Faris and H. Warren Dunham, *Mental Disorders in Urban Areas,* based on work begun in 1930 but not published in book form until 1939. In this study the connection between social disorganization and rates of hospitalization for mental disorders was established in a somewhat more elaborate ecological and statistical examination.

Drawing from all of the first-commitment cases from 1922 through 1934 at the four state and eight private hospitals in the Chicago area, the investigators had more than 30,000 cases to form the basis of rates.

They were also able to make use of the basic data on the Chicago districts gathered during the decade and more of research by the various social-science departments at the University of Chicago. The result of their study was a more definitive statement of the connections between personal characteristics and disorganized conditions of the city than had been possible in previous studies.

Like the ecological studies in Chicago of delinquency, crime, vice, family disorganization, suicide, and other expressions of personal disorganization, the research on mental disorders revealed a strong tendency for the high rates to concentrate in disorganized areas. The range of rates was very large; for example, the rates for all disorders in all hospitals expressed as an annual average of first admissions per 100,000 population aged 15 and over, varied from a low of 48 to a high of 499. The highest rate was in subcommunity 74, the central business district containing some hotel and hobo areas. The next highest rate, 480, was found in an adjacent hobo and rooming-house area; and the third highest, 357, in a rooming-house area. All of the ten highest rates were in a contiguous group of central hobo, rooming-house, and slum areas. The lowest rates were in a somewhat crescent-shaped band consisting of residential districts on or near the edges of the city.

This high concentration of rates strongly suggested a causal connection between the conditions of life in the disorganized areas and the abnormal behavior that leads to hospitalization. This possibility was favored by the fact that the different psychoses, plotted separately, had great differentiation of rate patterns in the city.

The attempt to perceive the nature of such causal connections required methods other than map plotting, such as a considerable amount of case-study and of statistical treatment. The success of the search varied by psychosis, from no success at all in explaining the distribution of manic-depressive psychosis to a fairly complete success in accounting for the concentration of general paresis. This latter psychosis is the consequence of syphilitic infection of the central nervous system and is connected with social disorganization through the already mentioned distribution of commercialized prostitution in the hobo and rooming-house districts. For schizophrenia, the most frequent form of abnormality in the Chicago statistics of the time, only a partial explanation could be suggested.

The open-ended nature of the study of mental disorders later stimulated a considerable amount of research by investigators in other cities on the variation of frequency of abnormality in the population. Advance has been continuous, but the complexities of the problem have so far prevented definitive conclusions.

Burgess and Bogue formulated a general statement concerning the character of the Chicago studies of social disorganization. "The formulation of this approach, and its gradual elaboration into the status of a comprehensive theory of social change and social problems is one of the major accomplishments of the University of Chicago during the 1920's and early 1930's. It begins with the presumption that a social problem is a malady of society, but that it is social rather than organismic processes that are deranged and in a pathological state. It rejects the organismic analogy and declares that there are characteristic processes and interactions whereby individuals are socialized and social control and community organization is maintained. Whenever these processes and interactions are deflected and where morals and customs are violated, social problems arise. On the one hand individuals are incompletely or differentially socialized and on the other hand social solidarity and social control are weakened, so that both personal and social disorganization results. This theory was found to be highly useful in explaining many urban social problems."[11]

[11] *Contributions to Urban Sociology,* p. 488.

~⸨ VI ⸩~

The Development of
Social Psychology

The prominence of the urban ecology studies at Chicago to some extent obscured other important directions of development occurring in the same period. The atmosphere of adventure, exploration, and responsibility for opening up new directions of sociological research, however, supported work in a variety of other fields within sociology as well. In all of these areas the same tentative spirit prevailed; there was no attempt to defend a doctrine or to establish a school of thought. Other schools could be destructively criticized, but even here Ellsworth Faris liked to warn students that the best method was to "criticize by creating." Any student who indicated that he possessed final knowledge was likely to encounter Faris's sarcastic comment, "Evolution always culminates in the writer."

Among the most notable lines of progress is that which occurred in the field of social psychology. Students at Chicago in the 1920's never heard the term *symbolic interactionism* applied to their social psychology tradition and no member of the department either attempted to name it or encouraged such naming. Every consideration was given to open exploration, none to naming or defending doctrine.

The philosopher-psychologist John Dewey, formerly at Chicago, had done most to stimulate the early interest in psychology among the sociologists. Late nineteenth-century psychology had been unduly influenced by an attempt to account for human actions on the basis of animal physiology. The apparent success of the instinct theory in explaining animal behavior seemed to promise that the same mechanisms would provide the key to human actions. The dominant psychological tradition toward the end of the nineteenth century was one of detailed physiological study of the individual, with virtually no interest in his social relations. Laboratory observation of animal behavior found no role for imagery, and a tendency arose to ignore or even to deny imagination in the human, or at best to concede no function to it.

William James, it will be recalled, did not dispense with imagination, and J. Mark Baldwin also perceived its operation in the social self. Dewey, however, contributed a critical argument against the dismissal of the functional role of imagination in his 1896 paper, "The Reflex Arc Concept in Psychology," in which he showed the inappropriateness of the switchboard conception of the nervous system.[1] In that view the reflex arc began with an external stimulus which was a cause of the behavior to follow and proceeded along nerve paths to a switching center from which an impulse to act was sent along other nerve paths to the proper muscles, the action of which was the end of the process and the result of the stimulus. Perhaps this formulation could be considered adequate for some of the behavior of simpler animals—for example, the pecking behavior of hens—and even for some human responses, such as the sneeze, the startle, and the knee-jerk reflex. The issue, however, was whether all human behavior, including that involving consciousness, could profitably be explained in terms of such an automatic reflex arc.

The psychological processes of a child reaching for a candle present the issue. Dewey granted that in a rough, practical way of representing the events in these processes the sensation of light, coming first, would be the stimulus to the grasping response that follows. But this stimulus-response explanation is not psychologically adequate, for "Upon analysis, we find that we begin, not with a sensory stimulus, but with a sensori-motor coordination, the optical-ocular, and that in a

[1] The Dewey paper is reprinted as a chapter titled "The Unit of Behavior" in his *Philosophy and Civilization* (New York: G. P. Putnam's Sons, 1931).

certain sense it is the movement which is primary, and the sensation which is secondary, the movement of body, head, and eye muscles determining the quality of what is experienced. In other words, the real beginning is with the act of seeing; it is looking, and not a sensation of light." [2]

Throughout the child's activity of reaching for the candle both seeing and reaching are in constant interaction, reinforcing each other, helping each other out. The reaching is ineffective and will not work without the seeing, and the reaching, in turn, must both stimulate and control the seeing. "The eye must be kept upon the candle if the arm is to do its work; let it wander, and the arm takes up another task. In other words, we now have an enlarged and transformed coordination; the act is seeing no less than before, but it is now seeing-for-reaching purposes. There is still a sensori-motor circuit—one with more content or value, not a substitution of a motor response for a sensory stimulus." [3]

Thus, Dewey contended, the reflex arc concept fails to account for behavior in which consciousness occurs because it attempts to separate the sensory stimulus and the motor response as distinct mental existences, ". . . while in reality they are always inside a co-ordination and have their significance purely from the part played in maintaining or reconstructing the co-ordination; and secondly, in assuming that the quale of experience which precedes the 'motor' phase and that which succeeds it are two different states, instead of the last being always the first reconstituted, the motor phase coming in only for the sake of such mediation." [4]

Therefore the behavior is not actually an arc but a *circuit*, a continual reconstitution rather than a series of jerks put into action by events external to the organism itself. The stimulus is in reality neither completely prior nor external. A sudden loud noise, which registers later in the nervous system and finally stimulates flight, may seem to have the temporal separation of the reflex arc, but only if we ignore the status prior to hearing the sound. "If one is reading a book, if one is hunting, if one is watching in a dark place on a lonely night, if one is performing a chemical experiment, in each case, the noise has a very different mental value; it is a different experience. . . . the 'stimulus'

[2] *Ibid.*, pp. 234–235.   [3] *Ibid.*, p. 235.   [4] *Ibid.*, p. 236.

emerges out of co-ordination; it is born from it as its matrix; it represents as it were an escape from it." [5]

The interrelation of stimulus and response is shown further in an example of a child who has reached for bright lights with differing consequences, some of which were pleasant and others were not. In this case, as the reaching begins, the response and the stimulus are equally uncertain. The problem is to discover the right stimulus as well as the right response. "The question of whether to reach or to abstain from reaching is the question what sort of bright light have we here? Is it the one which means playing with one's hands, eating milk, or burning one's fingers? The stimulus must be constituted for the response to occur." [6] Consciousness is involved in experiencing the stimulus by reason of the uncertainty about the later stages of the coordinated action. Anticipating the movements that may occur, along with imagining their possible consequences or *respective values,* takes place before attention goes to seeing this particular kind of light. "It is the initiated activities of reaching, which, inhibited by the conflict in the co-ordination, turn round, as it were, upon the seeing, and hold it from passing over into further act until its quality is determined." [7]

The argument is summarized in the following statement: "The circuit is a co-ordination, some of whose members have come into conflict with each other. It is the temporary disintegration and need of reconstruction which occasions, which affords the genesis of, the conscious distinction into sensory stimulus on one side and motor response on the other. The stimulus is that phase of the forming co-ordination which represents the conditions which have to be met in bringing it to a successful issue; the response is that phase of one and the same forming co-ordination which gives the key to meeting these conditions, which serves as instrument in effecting the successful co-ordination. They are therefore strictly correlative and contemporaneous. The stimulus is something to be discovered; to be made out; if the activity affords its own adequate stimulation, there is no stimulus save in the objective sense already referred to. As soon as it is adequately determined, then and only then is the response already complete. Attainment of either, means that the co-ordination has completed itself.

[5] *Ibid.,* p. 238.   [6] *Ibid.,* pp. 244–245.
[7] *Ibid.,* p. 245. The cybernetics student may readily perceive the negative feedback principle here.

Moreover, it is the motor response which assists in discovering and constituting the stimulus." [8]

Bode has similarly written: "In the reflex act . . . the response is like the first in a row of upstanding bricks, which in falling knock down one another . . . In the case of conscious activity, on the other hand, we find a very different state of affairs. The arc is not first constructed and then used, but is constructed as the act proceeds; and this progressive organization is, in the end, what is meant by conscious behavior. If the course of a reflex act may be compared with traveling in a railroad train, the progress of a conscious act is more like that of a band of explorers, who hew their path and build their bridges as they go along. The direction of the act is not determined from without but from within; the end is internal to the process." [9] This view permitted consciousness to have a causal role in human behavior, and opened the way for exploration of the effects of self-consciousness in human interaction and organization.

In friendship and interaction Dewey, along with his Chicago colleague in the Department of Philosophy and Psychology George Herbert Mead, and their mutual friend at Michigan Charles H. Cooley, built up a structure of basic social psychology which had immediate appeal to the sociologists at Chicago. Thomas was early attracted to it, and Faris, who earned his doctorate in psychology at Chicago while Dewey was still there, later gave it central emphasis in the department. Faris's own contributions to it consisted of only a few suggestive papers published in the journals, among the best known of these were "Are Instincts Data or Hypotheses?" "The Nature of Human Nature," and "Of Psychological Elements." [10]

The Chicago sociologists were convinced that they were approaching a firmer reality on the basis of a social psychology that recognized that much of social behavior consists of the interaction, not merely of physiological organisms but of conscious selves, constructed in imagi-

[8] *Ibid.*, pp. 247–248.

[9] Boyd Bode, "Consciousness and Psychology," in John Dewey *et al., Creative Intelligence* (New York: Henry Holt and Co., 1917), pp. 238–239.

[10] The first and third articles appeared in the *American Journal of Sociology,* XXVII, 184–196, and XLII, 159–176. The second paper was presented at a meeting of the American Sociological Society and is published as Chapter 2 in *The Nature of Human Nature* (New York: McGraw-Hill Book Co., 1937), pp. 7–20.

nation through a social process in the manner outlined by Cooley and Mead. This explanation did not deny any known facts of scientific physiology; it appeared to be clear that the simple processes such as conditioning occurred among human beings as well as among rats and pigeons. But, as Cooley had written, the solid facts of *social* life are the imaginations we construct of persons, in contrast to simpler automatic processes that produce social organization among insects, fish, and sheep.

There was, however, no practice of ignoring other traditions. Other approaches to social psychology were thoroughly read and studied by the faculty and students at Chicago: Freud, the Gestalt psychologists, Floyd Allport and his fellow Behaviorists, and other theorists then prominent. Most members of the department faculty believed some aspects of their contributions were useful. Faris found helpful material in the Gestalt tradition, for example, and Burgess and Ogburn were hospitable to some Freudian ideas. In general, however, the social psychology development at Chicago constituted a major break from the physiological psychology that had earlier seemed to be so promising.

A particular feature of the Chicago development was the destructive attack on the instinct theory. In a path-breaking 1918 article the psychologist Knight Dunlap had started the overt questioning of the existence of instincts in man. The thought was next taken up by Faris in his 1918 paper on instinct. His refutation of the theory was made easy by the high degree of disagreement among psychologists on what particular instincts were possessed by the human; some listed only one or two, others ten, fifteen, thirty, or more. Descriptions of particular instincts, moreover, needed only to be quoted to provide their own refutation. A leading psychologist of the time, for example, had described a hunting instinct as follows: "To a small escaping object, man, especially if hungry, responds, apart from training, by pursuit, being satisfied when he draws nearer to it. When within pouncing distance, he pounces upon it, grasping at it. If it is not seized he is annoyed. If it is seized, he examines, manipulates and dismembers it, unless some contrary tendency is brought into action by its sliminess, sting or the like. To an object of moderate size and not offensive mien moving away from or past him man originally responds much as noted above, save that in seizing the object chased, he is likely to throw himself upon it, bear it to the ground, choke and maul it until it is completely subdued, giving then a cry of triumph."[11] Other psychologists accounted for the popularity of baseball as the instinctive need of prehistoric man to run, throw, and strike, and one educational psychologist even wrote of vestigal horsemanship instincts in the behavior of children on rocking horses.

Faris's rejection of instincts was an early stage in the general movement. Dewey had questioned the utility of the instinct concept in the human about the same time, and the influential and destructive volume by Luther L. Bernard, *Instinct: A Study in Social Psychology*, which appeared in 1924, was thorough and definitive in its criticism of all aspects of the concept as applied to the human.

The abolition of human instincts, however, did not immediately turn attention away from the search for motivational principles in physiology. A series of instinct substitutes held popularity for a time. Thomas's four wishes were in vogue for a decade or so at Chicago, and Burgess found them particularly appealing. Until the Faris paper of 1936, "Of Psychological Elements," the entire tendency to classify motives in this manner had not been flatly challenged. After a review of the various motivational schemes of this type, he presented the verdict as follows: "Perhaps the disagreements of the past three hundred years may be explained by assuming that the differences were due to the impossibility of the problem. Men could not agree on the elements because they do not exist. The assumption in all of them was that individuals constitute society. But if we assume that society produces personalities, then the elements of personality will be found, not in the individual self at all, but in the collective life of the people."[12] The recognition of the fatal weaknesses of early motivational doctrines at last made possible full scholarly attention to the social sources of motivation which have no direct connection with specific categories of physiological satisfaction.

Twenty-three years after Faris disposed of motivational elements,

[11] Quoted from Edward L. Thorndike's *Educational Psychology*, I, p. 40, in E. Faris, *The Nature of Human Nature* (New York: McGraw-Hill Book Co., 1937), p. 63.
[12] Ellsworth Faris, *op. cit.*, p. 187.

Robert W. White published a similar conclusion in his paper, "Motivation Reconsidered: The Concept of Competence," in the *Psychological Review*, LXVI (September, 1959). This contribution was apparently reasoned independently, since in White's bibliography of 100 titles, not one is from the tradition described above.

The final freedom from instinctivism and internal physiological determinism permitted sociologists to concentrate on more realistic causation involving a distinctly human element, the social self—a development based on the progressive discussions of Baldwin, Cooley, Mead, and others. Cooley amply developed the point that the individual is not the rewarding object of the sociologists' interest and effectively directed attention to study of the person as a creation of society. He wrote: "If we accept the evolutionary point of view we are led to see the relation between society and the individual as an organic relation. That is, we see that the individual is not separable from the human whole, but a living member of it, deriving his life from the whole through social and hereditary transmission as truly as if men were literally one body." [13] Holding that a separate individual is an abstraction unknown to experience and granting that society does not exist without individuals, he declared that "society" and "individuals" do not denote separable phenomena but are simply collective and distributive aspects of the same thing.

Cooley gave sociologists the concept of the *looking-glass self*, which would seem to be a self actively constructed in imagery, employing the cybernetic functioning of consciousness in the manner described by Dewey in the paper on the reflex arc concept mentioned previously. It appears, however, that until Mead offered his analysis of the probable process by which interaction makes possible this construction of a self, Cooley did not fully realize the implication of his own concept because he rather casually expressed the opinion that the "emotion or feeling of self may be regarded as instinctive" and that it "seems to exist in a vague though vigorous form at the birth of each individual," although it could be developed by experience. Thus it remained for Mead to contribute a specific way in which an individual who is not

[13] Charles Horton Cooley, *Human Nature and the Social Order* (New York: Charles Scribner's Sons, 1902), p. 35.

born with a self may construct one in a social process, a contribution to social psychology for which Mead is most appreciated.[14]

As Mead saw it, lower animals do not have selves but they interact and may have a social process based on a *conversation of gestures*. Two dogs may snap and snarl at one another, the advance of one becoming a stimulus to the other's response, a retreat. The retreat may then become a stimulus for further action on the part of the first dog, and so on.

The same process, of course, may take place between humans, but there is another and more complex form of human interaction which does not occur among lower animals. The distinctly human *significant symbol* differs from the dog gestures in the important respect indicated by Dewey in his discussion of the reflex arc and the function of consciousness. In this phenomenon, the gesturing person responds to his own gesture in its early stages or to an inhibited gesture. The response may then function from the beginning to guide the course of the developing gesture. As Mead stated: "The function of the gesture is to make adjustment possible among the individuals implicated in any given social act with reference to the object or objects with which that act is concerned; and the significant gesture or significant symbol affords far greater facilities for such adjustment and readjustment than does the non-significant gesture, because it calls out in the individual making it the same attitude toward it (or toward its meaning) that it calls out in the other individuals participating with him in the given social act, and thus makes him conscious of their attitude toward it (as a component of his behavior) and enables him to adjust his subsequent behavior to theirs in the light of that attitude." [15]

There is, of course, no certainty that each person's response to his own gesture will be exactly like that of the other person. To the extent that they live in a common universe of discourse there would ordinarily be much similarity, but no social process guarantees against misun-

[14] George Herbert Mead, *Mind, Self and Society* (Chicago: University of Chicago Press, 1934). The date of the book is misleading because Mead died in 1931. The book was put together by his students and colleagues based on the notes taken in his course on Advanced Social Psychology as it evolved over many years. Mead spoke repetitively, without notes, and seemed to be thinking through the subject as he spoke.

[15] *Ibid.*, p. 46.

derstandings. Social interaction inevitably includes confusion as well as consensus.

The cybernetic functioning of consciousness, as outlined by Dewey and employed by Mead, makes possible the substitution of a trial–and–error process in imagination for an overt trial–and–error process, with its costly requirements of time and energy and its possible penalties for error. One commences a gesture in a tentative inhibited way, responds to it presumably as another would respond, and redirects the unfolding action according to the judgment of the imagined consequences, thereby gaining in efficiency. The same sort of response gives meaning to language. "You ask somebody to bring a visitor a chair. You arouse the tendency to get the chair in the other, but if he is slow to act you get the chair yourself. The response to the vocal gesture is the doing of a certain thing, and you arouse that same tendency in yourself. You are always replying to yourself, just as other people reply." [16]

According to Mead, objects become a part of our experience by virtue of their potential meaning in our activity. Each object becomes defined by our potential behavior toward it. "If one asked what the idea of a dog is, and tried to find that idea in the central nervous system, one would find a whole group of responses which are more or less connected together by definite paths so that when one uses the term 'dog' he does tend to call out this group of responses. A dog is a possible playmate, a possible enemy, one's own property or somebody else's. There is a whole series of possible responses. There are certain types of these responses which are in all of us, and there are others which vary with the individuals, but there is always an organization of the responses which can be called out by the term 'dog.' So if one is speaking of a dog to another person he is arousing in himself this set of responses which he is arousing in the other individual." [17]

Each person becomes a self, "an object to himself," according to the same principle. There is no direct intuition that reports to each of us what kind of object he is. "The individual experiences himself as such, not directly, but only indirectly, from the particular standpoints of other individual members of the same social group, or from the gener-

[16] *Ibid.*, p. 67.   [17] *Ibid.*, p. 71.

alized standpoint of the social group as a whole to which he belongs. For he enters his own experience as a self or individual, not directly or immediately, not by becoming a subject to himself, but only in so far as he first becomes an object to himself just as other individuals are objects to him or in his experience; and he becomes an object to himself only by taking the attitudes of other individuals toward himself within a social environment or context of experience and behavior in which both he and they are involved." [18]

Thus, Mead continues, "The self, as that which can be an object to itself, is essentially a social structure, and it arises in social experience. After a self has arisen, it in a certain sense provides for itself its social experiences, and so we can conceive of an absolutely solitary self. But it is impossible to conceive of a self arising outside of social experience." [19]

The self is actively put together in a social process employing imagination. It is a generalized construct made of interpretations of experience in interaction with other persons. Since other persons do not respond to each of us in the same way, we tend to acquire a somewhat different self toward each, but there may also be some generalization of the various selves that differ from person to person and group to group, based on the organization of our responses to what Mead called the *generalized other.*

The most original aspect of Mead's account was undoubtedly this detailed depiction of a way in which the most important determiner of human behavior, the self-concept, arises in a social process and comes into a human organization from outside. The human, physiologically among the most helpless and dependent creatures in the animal kingdom, thus obtains an emergent power which makes him the dominant species on earth. The physiological ability which makes this self-concept possible is the elaboration of the central nervous system which allows imagery and gives him the exceptionally complex cybernetic control of his actions before and during their expression. But the physiological ability alone does not suffice to produce the social self or the society. To the individual human being, society is there first, and by internalizing its processes, he acquires a mind, a supply of objects, a self, and a social world.

[18] *Ibid.,* p. 138.   [19] *Ibid.,* p. 140.

It is not difficult to see why this line of thought from Dewey, Cooley, and Mead would have special appeal to sociologists. Perhaps it would have spread even more rapidly were it not for the slow rate of publication by both Mead and Faris, who, along with Herbert Blumer and others, transmitted the organized thought to many hundreds of students through their annual lectures but made little of it available otherwise. Nevertheless, their important thoughts have survived and spread and in recent years have reached the stage of testing by modern research methods, both in the fields of sociology and psychology. In general the verification has been slow, but as far as the process has been tested, the above viewpoint has stood up well.

⟶(VII)⟶

The Range of Chicago Sociology

As the broad contents of the Park and Burgess text suggest, the intention at Chicago was to cover, as well as the small faculty could manage, the whole field of sociology. The conspicuous emphasis on urban studies resulted from using a geographic opportunity and the vigorous development of social psychology was partly a consequence of having Dewey and Mead on the campus. Ecology and psychology combined with much of the teaching and research in other branches of sociology, however, and these disciplines were at all times actively and purposefully interrelated. Some of the areas within the science of sociology receiving special attention at Chicago are discussed below.

The roots of sociology extend deep into cultural anthropology. William I. Thomas developed the interest in the early department at Chicago through his course and book on *Social Origins*. Faris continued this course after Thomas's departure and soon initiated an anthropology department by bringing in Fay Cooper Cole. After the department split, many sociology students continued to take courses in anthropology, and for some time the relations between the departments remained mutually stimulating. At Chicago and elsewhere general works in sociology drew abundantly from ethnological literature, and some of the leading cultural anthropologists maintained a close connection with relevant developments in sociology.

The ethnographic studies by Robert Redfield reflect an especially rich connection with sociology. Redfield, a son-in-law of Park, had begun a career as a lawyer but did not enjoy the work. Park suggested to him that he go into anthropology, then a part of the sociology department. In doing so, Redfield combined the Park influence with his own anthropological interests. Thus Park's sociology became clearly reflected in the series of Mexican community studies by Redfield, whose book *Folk Culture of Yucatan* is dedicated to Park. In addition to describing the communities he studied, Redfield had apparently hoped to derive knowledge with some sociological generality. (A letter from Park gave him some comprehension of the concept of the ideal type, which impressed Redfield so strongly that he wrote "Historic" on the sheet.) Redfield's research on Mexican communities appeared to be an attempt to discover useful ideal types of communities in the sense used by Park.

The concept of the ideal type also had a strong appeal for another of Park's students, Howard Becker, who published extensive generalizations on types of societies, with special application of the concepts of *sacred* and *secular* societies. These concepts had been richly treated in Park's courses.

Park regularly encouraged his students to undertake general but intensive studies of particular communities, attempting to perceive a community as a whole. Students undertook term papers and theses of this type, and some of them carried the practice into their classes at other universities. Jesse Steiner, an early student of Park, published twenty such studies, mostly of small towns, in *The American Community in Action* (New York: Henry Holt & Co., 1928). Albert Blumenthal later published a book, *Small Town Stuff* (Chicago: University of Chicago Press, 1932), on a mining village in the Rocky Mountain region. Like Redfield, his aim was to describe a particular small town in such a way as to bring out the ideal type. The conspicuous feature, as he saw it, was the richness of interpersonal acquaintanceship, close personal knowledge of the affairs of neighbors, and resulting pervasive social control in the small town. All this work is related by contrast to Park's interest in the stranger and to such studies of the impersonality of the rooming-house districts in the city as Zorbaugh's *The Gold Coast and the Slum.*

Park's doctoral dissertation at Heidelberg had been concerned with mass behavior, and in 1904 he had published *Masse und Publikum.* There was general sociological and psychologial interest in crowd behavior and revolution at Chicago and Park regularly encouraged research in the subject. One of his most popular courses, in fact, was The Crowd and the Public.

It would be easy to conceive crowd behavior and revolutionary action to be the antithesis of sociology—as chaos without possibility of explanation—but sociologists looked for natural processes in the interaction of members of the crowds and for the broader developments of which crowd activity is a regular phase. Park came to look for a general pattern that would apply to movements as different as political revolutions and religious movements, and he encouraged research of the type he called *natural history*. This latter concept differed from ordinary history in directing attention toward the typical rather than the unique. Thus a natural history of revolution would look for all aspects which tend to occur in revolutions generally, so that an ideal type of revolution could be described (ideal type again meaning the most representative, and not necessarily the most desirable).

Such a study was *The Natural History of Revolution* by Lyford Edwards (Chicago: University of Chicago Press, 1927), which compared a series of political revolutions. Although each revolution had unique features, certain typical stages tended to occur. Later historians—including Crane Brinton, who published *The Anatomy of Revolution* in 1938, and Louis Gottschalk, who published variously on the French Revolution—appeared to find essentially similar stages, although not independently, since they referred to Edwards's work.

Carl A. Dawson, also influenced by Park, carried the concept of stages into an analysis of the natural history of the Methodist movement, drawing his materials from standard historical sources. He saw the life cycle of this movement in such natural stages as the stage of unrest and contagion, the popular stage involving crowd excitement, the stage of formal organization, and the institutional stage. This cycle is similar to the general pattern observed in a large number of other religious movements as well as political revolutions.

The religious sect was also studied from other standpoints, such as the ethnographic description of varying social systems and as the effects of a social order on the processes of social psychology. As Ellsworth Faris wrote, "The sect is composed of sectarians and the sectarian is a personality. Moreover, his personality issues from the life of the sect and can be understood only if we take into account the social matrix in which it took form." [1] He also suggested that the sect provides useful material for the study of leadership, in view of the exceptional success of some leaders of sects in defining the society they create. A considerable number of term papers, a few theses, and the previously mentioned book on the Molokans of Los Angeles by Pauline V. Young followed this line of interest.

E. W. Burgess took over from C. R. Henderson the responsibility for developing the sociology of the family, and he continued to build this subject through his entire career. His scholarly interest covered the whole range of materials, including the ethnographic, but his attention centered on interaction patterns within the family and on the general change in form and function of the American family in the twentieth century. He referred to this change in the family as the transition from "institution to companionship."

Henderson's interest in sociology, as stated previously, was more heavily mixed with humanitarian motives than was that of his colleagues and successors, and only one doctoral dissertation, that of Earle E. Eubank, *A Study of Family Desertion* (1915), appears to have resulted from his instruction on the sociology of the family. The first doctoral research on the family under Burgess's influence was that of Ernest R. Mowrer, whose 1924 thesis title *Family Disorganization— An Introduction to a Sociological Analysis,* proclaimed it to have something more than a welfare concern. Mowrer's interest lasted throughout his academic career and was expressed in many books and articles, some in collaboration with his wife Harriet R. Mowrer.

Burgess's collaboration with Leonard S. Cottrell took a direction new to family sociology. Cottrell's 1933 doctoral dissertation, *The Reliability and Validity of a Marriage Study Schedule,* was a step on the way to a series of contributions toward the possibility of a statistical prediction of happiness in marriage. Using a method similar to one already developed by Burgess and some of his students for statistical prediction of success or failure of those on parole, these investigators developed an instrument which could be applied to an engaged couple to yield a score of predicted happiness of their intended marriage. The instrument was widely applied and then tested in

[1] *The Nature of Human Nature* (New York: McGraw-Hill Book Co., 1937), p. 47. The statement was actually written in the 1920's and republished in this collection of the author's papers.

follow-up studies. Some success in prediction was indicated at extremes of the scale, but prediction in the middle range was less successful. Rather than feel disappointed in the moderate utility of such an instrument, one must remember that what appears unsuccessful prediction may rather be success by human beings in controlling their lives; it is an indicator of freedom.

Other studies of the family produced theses on changing functions of the family, on variations of children by birth order, and on racial variations of family form, notably E. Franklin Frazier's dissertation *The Negro Family in Chicago* (1931) and his book *The Negro Family in the United States* (1939). Research in the 1940's by Robert Winch carried the Burgess interest into issues of personality interaction in courtship and led to Winch's interesting and somewhat controversial argument in defense of complementary differences as a basis of solidarity of engaged and married couples.

The culmination of the Burgess work on the family was his textbook in collaboration with Harvey J. Locke, *The Family: From Institution to Companionship.*[2] As the title states, the book is built around the sociological thesis that a broad change has been taking place in family styles from one institutionalized in formal and authoritarian law and mores, public opinion, tradition, and ritual to a companionship form of family with a unity based more on the specific relations between personalities, such as mutual affection, sympathetic understanding, and comradeship. The theme is developed with materials on family life in different societies, on the family and personality development, and on family organization, disorganization, and reorganization.

Although the Burgess-Locke book is the achievement of its authors, its valuable relation to the entire tradition in the Chicago department is symbolized by the acknowledgments in the preface. For the theoretical standpoint, the authors express indebtedness to Cooley, Faris, Mead, Park, and Thomas, although they add that in their analysis of the emotional aspects of interpersonal relationships within the family they have relied largely on the work of psychiatrists. Former students who read part or all of the manuscript and gave suggestions included Ruth S. Cavan, E. Franklin Frazier, Leonard S. Cottrell, Jr., Ernest R. Mowrer, Norman S. Hayner, and others.

[2] Ernest W. Burgess and Harvey J. Locke, *The Family: From Institution to Companionship* (New York: American Book Co., 1945).

Among his other concerns, Ogburn also had an interest in the changing aspects of family life, arising from his general research on the nature of social change. He early collaborated with Groves on a general book published in 1928, and later he included a section on the family in his noted collaborative study of social trends.[3] In addition, he contributed various articles on the subject over many years. Ogburn thus furnished important statistical support to general observations already familiar to sociologists.

Among the changes in the family shown by Ogburn were five:

1. The family has declined as an economic unit, not only in production, which has long been increasingly taken over by factories and shops, but also in housekeeping labor, which has been reduced by the increase in prepared foods, laborsaving mechanisms for the household, materials of home construction, furnishings which require less labor to maintain, and other factors, including employment of married women outside the home.
2. The protective function of the family has declined as firearms in the home have been replaced by organized police protection. The necessity for other family protection measures has been similarly reduced by fire departments, health departments, insurance companies, government security programs, and similar measures.
3. The educational function of the family has given way to external educational provisions, including school systems, nursery schools, vocational training organizations, and many facilities for private instruction in sports, music, and hobbies.
4. Much of the recreational function of the family has been displaced from the home through the increase in such facilities as playgrounds, golf courses, skating rinks, stadia for various sports, and motion picture theaters, and as a result, families have less recreation together.
5. The family's religious behavior has also changed, with an observable decline of three religious practices—families attending church together, reading the Bible at home, and saying grace at meals.

[3] Ernest R. Groves and William F. Ogburn, *American Marriage and Family Relationships* (New York: Henry Holt & Co., 1928); and William F. Ogburn and Clark Tibbitts, "The Family and Its Functions," Chapter 13 in *Recent Social Trends in the United States* (New York: McGraw-Hill Book Co., 1933).

The Chicago sociologists did not view these changes as portents of the disappearance of the family but rather as its adaptation to a changing world. The Burgess-Locke text points out that some important affectional and cultural functions of the family have remained during the period when other changes have been rapid.

As indicated above, Park entered sociology partly on the basis of an interest in crowd and mass behavior, and he kept the interest alive by his frequently taught course, The Crowd and the Public. Because no direct research on crowd behavior was then available, his materials were necessarily taken from scattered descriptions, rarely by sociological scholars, of various forms of collective behavior.

In the nature of the case, sociological research on crowd behavior is difficult to conduct because crowd activity is impractical to arrange and difficult to predict and ordinarily requires a staff and techniques beyond the reach of dissertation research. During Park's career at Chicago only two Ph.D. theses, judging from their titles, contained any detectable amount of collective-behavior material. These two were the 1924 thesis by Ernest T. Hiller, *The Strike as Group Behavior*, and the 1929 thesis by Thomas C. McCormick, *Rural Unrest*. A later M.A. thesis by Ethel Shanas, completed in 1938 after Park's retirement, dealt directly with the subject—*Nature and Manipulation of Crowds*.

Park's interest in collective behavior was not neglected, however. Students continued to absorb the subject with interest and respect and kept the material alive in the courses they taught in other colleges and universities, and in subsequent textbooks. In 1939 Herbert Blumer published a concise outline of the Park materials on collective behavior,[4] and in 1957 Ralph H. Turner and Lewis M. Killian, students of Blumer, amplified and modernized the tradition in their general textbook on *Collective Behavior*.[5]

Eventually a moderate amount of systematic research on collective behavior was attempted at Chicago and elsewhere. Some of this material consisted of disaster studies conducted by research teams distrib-

---

[4] Herbert Blumer, "Collective Behavior," Chapter 19 in Robert E. Park (ed.), *An Outline of the Principles of Sociology* (New York: Barnes and Noble, Inc., 1939), pp. 221–280.

[5] Ralph H. Turner and Lewis M. Killian, *Collective Behavior* (Englewood Cliffs, New Jersey: Prentice-Hall, Inc., 1957).

uted about the country who were prepared to move to the scene of any emergency and to make systematic observations of such collective behavior as it occurred. Events other than disasters have also provided opportunities for systematic observation, notably the study by the Langs and fellow students on the behavior of street audiences at a planned celebration in Chicago on the occasion of General MacArthur's return from military service in Korea.[6] An important finding of this MacArthur Day study was that newspapers, radio, and television can, on occasion, transmit the impression of wild crowd excitement when very little occurs. In view of the similar uncontrolled sources of most historical information on crowd phenomena, some doubt is cast on the objectivity of all descriptions not made by trained observers, and this means nearly all of the literature on collective behavior before very recent years.

The subject of race relations was of interest to most members of the Chicago department in the early 1920's. Because of his earlier association with Booker T. Washington, Park had a strong interest in all aspects of Negro race relations which broadened into a scholarly interest in the sociology of race relations all over the world. Faris, from his missionary experience in Africa, experienced a parallel development. Wirth's interest in the subject began with his studies of the ghetto and widened in a similar natural extension. Even Burgess was marginally involved in the subject through his part in advising such studies as Frazier's thesis on *The Negro Family in Chicago.*

The extensive concern, not only among scholars but by the public as well, in immigration and the problems resulting from it was another source of sociological interest in race and ethnic relations. *The Polish Peasant* study was directly based on this interest, and W. I. Thomas influenced both Park and Burgess to continue the line of inquiry. Burgess early made an investigation of the Russian peasant and in the 1930's made a trip to Russia for general observation. Thomas also had a part in instigating the research on acculturation that Park and Miller published.[7]

Burgess and Bogue have recently summarized the nature of this

[6] Kurt Lang and Gladys Engel Lang, "The Unique Perspective of Television," *American Sociological Review*, XVIII, (February, 1953), 3–12.

[7] Robert E. Park and Herbert Adolphus Miller, *Old World Traits Transplanted* (New York: Harper & Bros., 1921).

approach to ethnic research: "The discovery that the ethnic community was a gigantic sociological defense mechanism which facilitated
the survival and adjustment of immigrants but which the second
generation sought to modify and escape was a major research accomplishment of urban sociology during the 1920's and 1930's. . . . this
work was . . . analytical and concentrated on exploring the behavior
patterns and processes of adjustment and change as the immigrant
adapted to the new economic environment, and prospered. Stonequist's article on the marginal man is prototypical of the search that
was made for theoretical formulations. Wirth's study of *The Ghetto* set
a superb pattern for the sociological study of ethnic contrasts and
cultural change. Hostility and tension between ethnic groups were
treated as objective phenomena to be explained rather than a battle to
be joined."[8]

From Simmel, under whom he had studied, Park acquired the
concept of social distance. This notion appeared to have promise in
the research on race and ethnic relations, and he suggested to Emory
Bogardus that the latter devise a social-distance scale as a statistical
basis for the life-history materials in this field. The result was the well-
known Bogardus scale, which introduced a principle elaborated in the
Cornell scaling methods developed much later by Louis Guttman and
others.

Elaborating other thoughts acquired from Simmel, Park speculated
at length about the various types and degrees of separation from
community life and encouraged research on the migrant, the stranger,
and the ethnic type he called the *marginal man,* who had transitional
membership in more than one group but no full and satisfying membership in any. Park's contributions on this subject were transmitted in
detail to his student, Everett Stonequist, for the latter's doctoral dissertation and the book which appeared a few years later.[9] One result of
the introduction of this concept was that the experience of any particular ethnic group could be understood as a result of general sociological processes rather than as unique misfortunes of its particular
history. An expected consequence was the reduction of emotional

---

[8] Park and Miller, *op. cit.,* p. 325.
[9] Everett Stonequist, *The Marginal Man* (New York: Charles Scribner's Sons,
1937).

agitation in the discussions of race relations, a necessary spirit for any scientific development of knowledge.

Research in the same directions, influenced by Park, included the study of the Molokans of Los Angeles by Pauline V. Young, the researches in Hawaii by Andrew W. Lind and by Clarence Glick, and the studies of ethnic relations in the province of Quebec by Everett C. Hughes and by Horace Miner.[10] Research by a younger generation of Chicago students, Shirley Star, Morris Janowitz, S. Frank Miyamoto, and Dietrich Reitzes, penetrated new subject matter in the same general spirit.

Park's newspaper experience influenced him in several ways. Undoubtedly it was a factor in his emphasis on vigorous firsthand data gathering, which had not been a feature of nineteenth-century sociology. This experience extended the range of his interests into aspects of human life overlooked in the relatively restricted concerns of some early sociologists. It was also an incentive to develop in sociology a responsibility for research into the nature and formation of public opinion and into the newspaper itself as it influenced opinion.

A few term papers in Park's courses were written on matters relating to public opinion. The two students principally interested in the newspaper itself, however, were Helen MacGill Hughes (wife of Everett C. Hughes) and Carroll D. Clark.

While it was characteristic of Park to have close friendships with his students and to give generously of time and ideas which they could use in their dissertations and books, no students were as close to him, and for as long a time, as were Everett and Helen Hughes. In an important sense, these two are the students who have carried the most Park influence, although both have also contributed their own progress and originality to the material they obtained from their teachers. Helen Hughes took Park's courses in the middle 1920's and during that time pursued her study of the human interest aspect of the news. The Ph.D. thesis, *News and the Human Interest Story,* was completed

---

[10] Among the titles of particular interest are: Andrew W. Lind, *An Island Community* (Chicago: University of Chicago Press, 1938); Everett C. Hughes, *French Canada in Transition* (Chicago: University of Chicago Press, 1943); and Horace Miner, *St. Denis: A French-Canadian Parish* (Chicago: University of Chicago Press, 1939).

much later, in 1937, and a book bearing the same title appeared in 1940.[11]

The interest of American sociologists in the nature of social organization was stimulated in part by Durkheim's book on the division of labor. In *Folkways*, Sumner spoke of the structure of institutions, and Cooley published an important general discussion of the sociology of organization.[12] Max Weber's work also was well-known to Park and Wirth and was read by those graduate students who could understand German, including Everett Hughes and Howard Becker. Ellsworth Faris, though mainly responsible for social psychology, never lost sight of the importance of formal organization and involved his students in the subject in their research on social movements and sects. In fact, in his 1932 paper, "The Primary Group: Essence and Accident," he specifically pointed to the need for attention to formal organization, stating: "This is not to say that the primary group is a value concept and therefore superior to other types of groups. Human institutions are erected to meet human needs, and these needs may sometimes be better satisfied by institutions than by primary group relations. Indeed, primary group relations may intrude in a disorganizing manner, as when a police officer refuses to arrest a man because he is a friend. Here belong much of the corruption, bribery, nepotism, and 'graft' of our modern life. Formal and institutional groups cannot perform their function unless the distinction between them and the primary group be kept with scrupulous clarity." [13]

Later Herbert Blumer also wrote forcefully of the importance of keeping clear distinctions between interaction processes operating in small primary groups and in large organizations, indicating the futility of attempting to understand industrial and race relations on the basis of interpersonal interaction. Writing of the studies of human relations in industry which had become popular among students of industrial processes, he criticized them as seeming to rest on the premise that "industrial relations are primarily direct relations between the people in the local plant or factory." Without denying that what takes place

[11] Helen MacGill Hughes, *News and the Human Interest Story* (Chicago: University of Chicago Press, 1940).

[12] Charles H. Cooley, *Social Organization* (New York: Charles Scribner's Sons, 1909).

[13] *American Journal of Sociology*, XXXVIII (July, 1932), 46.

"on the front line of contact between worker and supervisor" is of importance, he argued that the more important processes are those of the organizational level. Unionization, and particularly industrial unionization, incorporates workers into organizations of vast dimensions, and their relation to management is increasingly mediated by such organizations. Relations between worker and manager become relations between two large organizations, and the processes and principles that operate in this interaction are of a character which has no resemblance to those of person-to-person interaction.[14]

Park, busy with other subjects, nevertheless was sensitive to the importance of the study of organization and stimulated it as the opportunity became available. His student and close friend Everett Hughes later became a principal developer at Chicago of this direction of interest. His 1928 doctoral dissertation, *A Study of a Secular Institution: The Chicago Real Estate Board,* was not only a thorough case study of the growth of a particular formal organization but also a rich and complete discussion of the general sociology of organization. Perhaps as characteristic of Park's students, Hughes actually started his research with study of the ecology of real-estate values in Chicago and eventually developed an interest in the Real Estate Board as an example of the growth of a particular organization. This interest led him into a long career of studying organization in general and a variety of specific organizations and the processes within them. In the course of these studies Hughes provided apprenticeship, training, and stimulation to a large number of younger students who also became productive in this area of sociology.

The topic of organization has a good claim to being the heart of sociology. The most important characteristic of the human is that the individual is formed and controlled by his fellow man, and the greater part of this influence comes through organized social relations. Earlier theorists had perceived the existence of institutions and organizations, but for the most part they tended to see them as elaborations of individual needs or motives. It remained for the twentieth-century writers to develop the thought, well expressed in the aphorism of John Dewey, that the instincts do not produce the institutions, but rather the institutions produce the instincts.

[14] Herbert Blumer, "Sociological Theory in Industrial Relations," *American Sociological Review,* XII (June, 1947), 271–278.

But if organization is not a consequence of the original nature of the individual members, the question immediately emerges—What produces the organization? The answer appears to be that it arises in a process of interaction in which individual intention, foresight, or planning is not necessarily the determining influence. Apparently a *need* or *function* can exist which is a requirement not of an individual, nor of a group of individuals, but of a collectivity of a higher order.

In the introductory chapter of his thesis Hughes wrote that the Real Estate Board grew, as did many other organizations, not from a grand dream of a desired future, but from daily emergencies. Its growth, like that of Lloyds, the London insurance house, did not stem from a single broad decision. Quoting from a history of that firm, he characterized the process as follows: "At no time, so far as we are aware, did any group of men say to each other: Go to; let us make the greatest centre of insurance in the world. Even association waited for well over a century, and incorporation for nearly two centuries. Certain men took their seats at a coffee-house table, and pledged themselves individually, for a consideration, to take upon themselves the perils of the sea, men-of-war, fire, enemies, pirates, thieves, etc., with all other perils which might come to the hurt or detriment of the subject-matter of insurance . . . It is a striking example of evolution as distinguished from creation."

Hughes went on to state: "The Chicago Real Estate Board began more consciously and with a definite purpose. Programs of legislation have been projected and pursued assiduously for years on end; but they have had to do with pressing problems rather than with eternal principles. No group of men deliberately planned the present character and policy of the institution on the basis of given premises. Its character developed as a by-product of its activity."

What Hughes accomplished in his thesis was to document in detail the ways in which the day-to-day problems called forth practical responses to deal with them, while organizational structure imperceptibly grew over the years and decades, becoming ever more complex but not disordered. In fact, a consistency that could be thought of as *organizational wisdom* steadily evolved, and in other ways the institution acquired a character of its own that could hardly be deduced from a sum or average of the character of the persons involved in its processes.

Floyd Allport and others attempted to refute this kind of sociology as it was developing in the 1920's by claiming that an organization could be no more than the sum of individuals and that any statement conflicting with this would constitute mysticism. But there is a sense in which it is more realistic to say that organizations are not composed of persons as the basic units or elements, but rather of parts, or aspects, of persons. The ant or the bee may belong to his colony or hive with all his being, but the human is versatile enough to belong to several organizations but not necessarily to each with his whole character. The separation of *roles* and *offices* allows for the sociologically real argument that organizations may be composed of these as the elements. The bank is composed of bank officers, not whole persons. Outside of business hours the same persons may be husbands, fathers, club members, and clowns. These latter roles do not constitute any part of the banking organization.

The sociology of organization thus elaborates into the study of roles, careers, professions, and occupational types, as well as of a variety of specific organizations. Hughes and his students have expanded knowledge in all of these areas, and continue to do so at an accelerated pace forty years after his dissertation on the Chicago Real Estate Board.

In a real sense all good sociology is sociological theory, and most sociologists have needed some knowledge of the history of the subject. Among the few who have chosen to give special attention to the historical and speculative aspects of their science was Louis Wirth. German-born and fluent in the German language, he had a particularly rich familiarity with German contributions to sociology. He wrote an early article to summarize the contributions of Tönnies, and with Edward Shils translated Karl Mannheim's *Ideology and Utopia* in 1936. In a year abroad in 1930 and 1931 he made the acquaintanceship of Mannheim, as well as Sombart, Leopold von Wiese, and other German sociological scholars. Wirth's European familiarity, in fact, led to an important role in the establishment of the International Sociological Association, and in 1950 he became its first president.

William F. Ogburn came to the Chicago department from Columbia in 1927. He had been a student of Giddings and brought with him a respect for some of the substantive contributions of that teacher. More importantly, he imported Giddings's strong emphasis on the value of statistics as a tool for sociological research. Instruction in statistical methods had been available before that time, but only in other departments, and the utility of statistics was not fully recognized by the graduate students. However, all members of the department had a commitment to science and an appetite for method as was expressed in the techniques used in urban ecology, in crude efforts at statistics and scaling, and in the gathering of case studies and life histories.

Ogburn immediately increased the offerings of courses in statistics, and graduate students were promptly required to take some of this work. Tastes differed; while some students who feared the subject took minimal work, others devoured all they could get and even asked for more. Samuel A. Stouffer, for example, who turned to sociology from newspaper work, became so fascinated with statistics that he took all the courses he could get at Chicago, then studied mathematics, and finally went on to spend a year in England mainly studying new statistical techniques being developed by R. A. Fisher and his colleagues. Four years after his return, Stouffer became a professor in the Chicago department and a colleague of Ogburn; some years later he became a professor at Harvard and director of the Harvard Laboratory of Social Relations.

For a brief period in the late 1920's some of the faculty and students in the Chicago department reacted against the strong emphasis on statistics. There were debates at colloquia and over lunches on statistics versus the case-study method. Burgess and Blumer sometimes presented the arguments on the case-study side; Ogburn, his student and admirer Thomas C. McCormick, and Stouffer consistently defended the value of statistical methods. The argument waned in time, however, and Burgess attended Ogburn's statistics courses in 1928 and later made important use of statistical methods in his research. In his thesis research Stouffer virtually finished the argument by destroying one of the principal contentions of the case-study side.[15] This controversy concerned whether the scales devised to measure attitudes in order to treat them statistically really measured the same dimension that the skilled researchers who used the case studies and life histories had in mind.

To test this issue, Stouffer had hundreds of students write autobi-

---

[15] Samuel Andrew Stouffer, *An Experimental Comparison of Statistical and Case History Methods of Attitude Research* (Doctoral dissertation, University of Chicago, 1930).

ographies, instructing them to include everything in their life experiences relating to alcohol usage and the prohibition law. Each of these autobiographies was read by a panel of persons presumed to be qualified in life-history research, and for each subject the reader indicated on a scaled line the position of the subject's attitude regarding prohibition. Interreader agreement was found to be satisfactory.

Each of the same subjects had also filled out a questionnaire that formed a scale of the Thurstone type. The close agreement of the scale measurement of each subject's attitude with the readers' estimate based on the life history indicated that, as far as the scale score was concerned, nothing was gained by the far more lengthy and laborious process of writing and judging a life history.

The use of case studies did not disappear, however; merely the argument that they made statistics unnecessary. Ogburn himself spoke favorably of the value of case studies in providing suggestions for hypotheses which could then be tested by more formal methods, including statistics. The two approaches became complementary rather than rival.

Ogburn was also influential in stimulating interest in the study of population which expanded and flourished through the later work of Stouffer, Hauser, Duncan, and others. In time population study came to be interrelated with urban studies and ecology, thus completing a partial resolution of the separate interests of Park and Ogburn which had earlier appeared to have rival status.

Social change was another interest brought in by Ogburn. Thomas and later Faris had for some years taught Social Origins, a course which dealt with broad aspects of whole societies and with evolutionary periods. Ogburn's interests centered on detailed mechanisms and processes that bring changes to society, and, influenced by a taste for economic determinism acquired at Columbia, he gave special attention to technological changes and particularly to inventions. His theory was stated in mature form in his first book on the subject and later greatly elaborated in *Recent Social Trends*.[16]

Ogburn's patient, thorough, and carefully reasoned treatment played an important part in changing the view of the importance of

---

[16] William F. Ogburn, *Social Change: With Respect to Culture and Original Nature* (New York: B. W. Huebsch, 1922); and William F. Ogburn, *Recent Social Trends in the United States* (New York: McGraw-Hill Book Co., 1933).

individual ability in the invention process. He did not deny that some amount of ability was necessary for invention, but he made a strong case for the far greater importance of what he called the *cultural base*, the existing complex of inventions and knowledge. He showed that each invention is only a small step, usually made by combining elements already present in the cultural base; no complex invention is ever made outright from nothing. For any new machine, such as the airplane, the radio, the automobile, the many small steps of invention were made by a large number of persons, few of them remembered in history. The attribution of an invention to a single inventor is a reflection of a public appetite for heroes more than a realistic statement of the origin of new things.

Ogburn wrote of three elements in the invention process: the inventor, the need, and the cultural base, but he argued that without the readiness of the cultural base, no degree of urgent need nor any available genius could produce the invention. Furthermore, when the cultural base is ready for an invention, it will soon occur. The case for this last point, perhaps the most original and important part of Ogburn's argument, is supported by a long list of inventions that were made independently and virtually simultaneously by two or more persons. Ogburn noted that the telegraph, telephone, phonograph, sewing machine, airplane, typewriter, and many other mechanical inventions had two or more inventors; simultaneous discoveries in science were also numerous. Later scholars made similar lists in special fields of science.

Consequently, the larger the cultural base, the greater are the possibilities for further invention. Thus it would be expected, as appears to be the case, that the historical trend in innovation has the general form of an exponential curve.

Ogburn's special interest in the contribution of technology to social change did not constitute a denial that nontechnical aspects of culture could also influence changes. Even so, his published work amounted to a strong case for the dominant role of the material culture in the historical development of civilization and the main directions and pace of change in contemporary life.

While his colleagues had been determined well before he joined the department to build a science and to devise methods that could be thought of as scientific, Ogburn furthered this growth. Through his teaching of statistical methods and his continued questioning, How do you know this? he stimulated his students to hasten the search for useful methods and to undertake a reexamination of the accumulated fund of sociology by applying this question and devising new tests. The Thomas-Park-Burgess-Faris work in the 1920's was to construct a plausible viewpoint and body of consistent sociological knowledge. Ogburn's most important long-term influence was to show the need for and the means to examine this attitude and information for its scientific soundness.

From time to time Ogburn published specific demonstrations of what statistical method could accomplish. Some of these were sophisticated interpretations of available statistical material; others used complex statistical analysis.

A characteristic example of the former kind is a study of major factors in the living standard of nations.[17] This work constituted a correction to a popular belief that the high standard of living in the United States is a consequence mainly of an abundance of natural resources. Ogburn compared five countries: China, India, the United Kingdom, the United States, and the Soviet Union with reference to four measures of factors considered to be related to standard of living. The factors were size of population, organization, natural resources, and density of population. The five nations all have abundant natural resources but greatly varying standards of living. No direct measures of organization is available, but Ogburn argued that a measure of technological development, while distinguishable from organization, would serve as a useful measure of it. The standard of living was measured by an average figure for what an hour of labor bought in each country.

The principal finding was that technology is by far the most important of the four factors; the correlation of technological development with the measure of standard of living was .7 for the five countries. The correlation with density, by contrast, was −.3; a similar relationship also found in a larger set of eighteen nations. Ogburn reflected in conclusion: "It is obvious that natural resources are a necessity for a high standard of living, but the question concerns their variability

[17] William F. Ogburn, "Population, Private Ownership, Technology, and the Standard of Living," *American Journal of Sociology*, LVI (January, 1951), 314–319.

from country to country, not their existence as a factor. Furthermore, technology is needed to use natural resources. Organization is also closely related to technology. One wonders, indeed, how much difference in economic organization there can be with the same technology, given a sufficiently long time to make adjustments and remove cultural lags."

A second example of Ogburn's ingenious methods is furnished by his partial correlation analysis of election issues in the presidential campaign of 1928, in which Herbert Hoover defeated Alfred E. Smith.[18] The question was important because of the later controversy about President Hoover's mandate and whether his election constituted a public assent to the Prohibition Amendment.

Ogburn required measurements for each issue. For voting units he used 173 counties widely spread over the nation but not including southern states. Five variables, representing issues in the election, were correlated with the per cent of the vote in each county cast for Smith, the Democratic Party candidate. These variables were: the foreign-born population, obtained from census figures; the per cent urban, also from the census; the per cent of adults who were Catholic (since Smith's membership in the Catholic Church was presumed to be an issue); the per cent voting wet (i.e., opposed to the prohibition of alcoholic beverages), obtained from a national magazine polling survey; and the per cent of voters regularly voting Democratic, obtained from a recent election without major issues in which the total vote might be considered to represent party membership.

Each issue was correlated with the Smith vote. The highest relationship, .65, was between the Smith vote and the wet vote. In order of size the other issues correlated with the Smith vote as follows: Catholic .47, foreign-born .33, urban .16, and Democratic .11. Thus the impression is that the wet issue and the religious issue were most important in determining the election, and that of regular party membership almost negligible.

But the variables are intertwined, since, for example, urban voters tend to be more opposed to prohibition than are rural voters and are also more likely to be Democratic and Catholic. It is necessary to untangle these factors in order to see the influence of each one sepa-

[18] William F. Ogburn and N. Talbot, "A Measurement of the Factors in the Presidential Election of 1928," *Social Forces*, XVIII (December, 1929).

rately. The untangling was done by partial correlation, in which the correlation coefficients are computed and the influence of all other factors is eliminated by their being held constant statistically.

With all other factors held constant, the highest relationship of the Smith vote is still to the wet vote, .56. Next in size again is the relation to the Catholic vote, .33. Third is the relation to the Democratic vote, .25 (more than twice as large as the uncontrolled correlation). The foreign-born vote showed the fourth-highest relation, .07. The urban vote presented a negative relationship of −.18; that is, the urban voter seemed to support Smith, but only seemed so because the urban voter was more likely to be Catholic, Democratic, and wet; when these influences were removed, the urban vote was somewhat *against* Smith.

When Ogburn computed a multiple correlation of correlation for the above issues, he obtained a figure of .77. The square of this, .59, estimates the proportion of variance measured, that is, it reports that the issues in the study accounted for something like 59 per cent of the issues that determined the election. The unmeasured 41 per cent is composed of other issues not taken into account and of crudity and error in the measurement of the issues used. Given the various difficulties in research on such matters as this, Ogburn's achievement must be considered as an exceptional display of the possibilities of statistical discovery.

The personalities of the sociologists discussed in this chapter were about as diverse as would normally be found in an academic department. They were assembled from varied backgrounds and had many differences in personal tastes. There was little homogeneity of personality to hold them together; their working harmony was the consequence of mutual confidence and a strong sense of the importance of what they were doing. The period of the 1920's, especially of the latter half, was characterized by an exceptionally high morale in the department among the faculty and the graduate students alike. Probably as many bases of personal conflict were present here as in most departments—there was in fact mutual antagonism among some wives—but this had no chance of growing into overt discord as long as the general progress of the teamwork was so apparent to all.

This same unity and morale was noticed by sociologists elsewhere and caused comparisons and even open resentment among scholars at other universities. Some saw the spread of Chicago-trained students into universities and department chairmanships around the country as tending toward a monopoly of sociological training, as well as a dangerous overproduction of sociologists. In 1934, Chapin published a brief statement of his concern on the latter point.[19] From a list of subscribers interested in obtaining positions and a list of doctoral dissertations in progress in the July 1933 *American Journal of Sociology*, he calculated that some 258 promising graduate students were aspiring for 130 positions in university departments of sociology, in which at the most only 5 per cent of the needed positions would be open each year. He estimated that in 1933 completed dissertations would be 17 times the number of estimated vacancies. Two universities, Chicago and Columbia, were said to have passed the "danger line," Chicago by a slight margin more than Columbia.

Ellsworth Faris published an immediate supplement to Chapin's note supplying a somewhat different perspective.[20] He pointed out that 30 per cent of the job-seeking persons listed in the Personnel Exchange were known to be employed and that many were still engaged in study. Furthermore, Chapin's list of opportunities included only major positions in universities with graduate training, while a variety of other opportunities were opening to persons with sociological training. In general, the experience of later years bore out this optimism for no extended period of unemployment of trained sociologists ever occurred, and the imbalance has eventually turned out to be a severe shortage with no end in sight even at the present time.

In the middle 1930's, however, the size and effectiveness of the Chicago influence in sociology began to appear to some as a power-seeking conspiracy. From the founding of the American Sociological Society in 1905 until 1936, its official journal, the *American Journal of Sociology*, was owned by the University of Chicago and always edited by a member of the Chicago faculty. The special advantage of this control of the journal seemed inappropriate. This sentiment, in fact, partly motivated the establishment of *The American Sociological Review*—a move which relieved feelings and at the same time provided

---

[19] F. Stuart Chapin, "The Present State of the Profession," *American Journal of Sociology*, XXXIX (January, 1934), 506–508.

[20] Ellsworth Faris, "Too Many Ph.D.'s?" *American Journal of Sociology*, XXXIX (January, 1934), 509–512.

needed additional publication space to the rapidly growing number of sociologists in America.

The minor rebellion in the American Sociological Society, which came to a climax at the annual convention in 1935, had a distinctly anti-Chicago character. Not only had the Chicago sociologists owned and dominated the official journal, but they had also appeared to a few members to hold undue influence in the affairs of the Society. In the preceding dozen years eight of the presidents had been associated with Chicago, either on the faculty or as students: Charles Ellwood (1923), R. E. Park (1925), W. I. Thomas (1927), W. F. Ogburn (1929), Emory Bogardus (1931), Luther L. Bernard (1932), E. B. Reuter (1933), and E. W. Burgess (1934). For several years also, the Secretary of the Society had been Herbert Blumer, then on the Chicago faculty. A group of members, caucusing, lobbying, and engaging in behind-the-scenes politicking, eventually succeeded in electing a non-Chicago secretary and establishing the *American Sociological Review*, but they failed in an effort to change the name of the Society.

Such political activity caused some of the leading members of the Society, not all of whom were Chicago men, to feel that the integrity of the Society was being threatened, particularly by making the election of its president a matter of contention instead of a conferral of honor and recognition. Furthermore, they felt that the Society was turning away from its traditional scholarly research character toward an active participation in national political and social controversy.

Such a concern led to the formation of the Sociological Research Association, an organization of limited membership specifically dedicated to a research interest and originally envisioned as a fortress to which the objective scholar might retreat if the American Sociological Society were to be diverted from its traditional purposes by the new regime. The SRA was first conceived of in a conversation in late 1935 between Herbert Blumer and R. D. McKenzie, then further discussed by a group which included E. B. Reuter, Stuart Rice, Kimball Young, Ellsworth Faris, George Lundberg, R. E. Park, and E. W. Burgess. In the spring of 1936 the SRA was organized at a meeting in Chicago attended by between forty and fifty sociologists from various parts of the country. The constitution limited the membership to one hundred and established a simple method of electing officers—one new member would be elected to a council of five each year, and in his fifth year the member would be president. New members of the SRA were to be admitted by majority vote of the entire membership in a mail ballot. The SRA survived, but it did not have occasion to become a substitute for the American Sociological Society. The character of the Society was not changed substantially by the developments described above and the SRA no longer needed to be conceived of as a standby in case of its failure. SRA survives as an almost functionless organization which holds a single dinner meeting each year at the time and place of the American Sociological Association convention.

The anti-Chicago revolt, of teacup dimensions in the perspective of longer history, dissolved with few traces. In 1937, 1939, and 1941 the presidents of the Society were Ellsworth Faris, E. H. Sutherland, and Stuart Queen, who were working at or trained at Chicago. There was, however, less of a feeling of imbalance in sociological influence than had existed in the earlier years.

~VIII~

The Leadership Competition

The Chicago department faculty that succeeded Small, Henderson, Vincent, and Thomas remained intact until about the middle 1930's. Park retired from Chicago in 1934 and then taught for two years more at Fisk University. Ellsworth Faris retired in 1939 and Ogburn in 1951. Wirth died prematurely in 1952. Burgess who retired from teaching at Chicago in 1951, died while this book was in publication. To a considerable extent the first replacements for these men came from the supply of Chicago-trained sociologists, among them Herbert Blumer, Samuel Stouffer, and Everett Hughes, who constitute a third generation.

The major accomplishments of the second generation in writing as well as teaching were made during their middle years. The depression of the 1930's and the war which followed brought distractions and disruptions to American scholarship in general. Nevertheless, the Chicago department remained large, productive, and influential. There is no history of a decline to relate, at least in absolute magnitude. The position of special dominance, however, so notable in the 1920's, inevitably faded as strong departments of sociology emerged at other universities. Leadership became ever more shared with Columbia as its department increased in size and power, and then with a number of expanding universities such as Michigan, Wisconsin, North Carolina, the University of California Los Angeles, and others. Harvard introduced sociology cautiously at first, importing Pitirim Sorokin and Carle C. Zimmerman, and later Talcott Parsons, who introduced and developed the subject until the vigorous growth after the Second World War. At that time Stouffer was brought in and a Department of Social Relations with a research laboratory went into operation. In the meantime able Chicago-trained men built up departments at a number of widely scattered campuses: E. T. Krueger at Vanderbilt, Walter C. Reckless at Ohio, Edwin H. Sutherland at Indiana, Leonard S. Cottrell at Cornell, E. B. Reuter at Iowa, R. D. McKenzie at Michigan, Carl A. Dawson at McGill, Jesse Steiner at Washington, Andrew W. Lind at Hawaii. Princeton eventually admitted sociology to its curriculum, as did California, and even later Johns Hopkins. Yale experienced a postwar recovery and the University of Washington expanded vigorously in the same period under the leadership of George Lundberg. American sociology was thus spread about the country so thoroughly that the dominant midwestern region, apart from Chicago, even began to display indications of feeling bypassed.

As the nineteenth century waned, it would have been difficult for a neutral scholar to predict successfully the direction sociology would take. There were predictions enough by the advocates of each direction. Giddings was sure that sociology must go in the direction he preferred, holding that it was impossible to go in any other way. Ward, Sumner, and other dominant figures for the most part showed strong confidence in what they considered the true direction. The explanation of the outstanding success at Chicago, however, requires some speculation on why Small's rivals for the leadership of American sociology were less successful in producing a living and growing tradition.

The relatively slight influence of Lester F. Ward is perhaps the easiest to explain. Although he has been called the father of American sociology, he left perhaps the least academic posterity of any of the sociologists prominent in his time. This is by no means to imply that his career was fruitless; Ward made important contributions to the sociological heritage, but as a distinguishable approach to sociology, his tradition faded a few years after his death.

Ward's career was unique; no student could follow in his footsteps. His wide knowledge of biology and his concern with evolution in its broadest sense gave him an appetite and ambition for universal knowledge that led one author to refer to him as "the American Aristotle." [1] One Aristotle does not duplicate himself in dozens of students and disciples, and Ward did not even achieve a second Ward. His principle lieutenant was James Q. Dealey, who succeeded Ward at Brown as head of the political and social science department, but Dealey failed to persuade the students and faculty at that university, as well as sociologists elsewhere, that the Ward approach to sociology led into the future. As late as 1939 E. A. Ross wrote as unrealistic a statement as one can devise about Ward, declaring, "After forty-six years of teaching sociology, I can testify that youth is swept off its feet by the big Wardian outlook." [2] At Brown sociology came close to extinction after some years of Dealey's unpopular emphasis on "telesis" and his doctrinaire thundering at the "interests," including John D. Rockefeller, who had made important gifts to the university and who, it was hoped, was willing to make more.

Ward's close friend and admirer E. A. Ross also enjoyed denouncing railroads, utilities, and malefactors of great wealth in the nineteenth-century populist spirit. He had personal reason for this, having been discharged from the Stanford faculty by the widow of Leland Stanford, that university's wealthy benefactor, for advocating views which appeared to her to be unsound and threatening.

Ross produced sociology and published enormous amounts of it. His textbook *Social Psychology* established an early sociological claim to that field, and his writings on social control, collective behavior, population problems, and many other subjects added much to the useful fund of sociological knowledge. But above all, Ross was concerned with action and reform, and so he tended to appeal more to impatient temperaments than to objective scholars. His department at Wisconsin grew and flourished, but his personal influence motivated students as much or more for progressive causes as it did for constructing a body of knowledge.

Neither Ward nor Ross appeared to have an effective interest in searching for methods of discovery and testing specifically useful in research problems of sociology. The scientific method appeared to be too slow for the urgent tasks that held their interest. Ross was among

---

[1] Samuel Chugerman, *Lester F. Ward, The American Aristotle* (Durham, N.C.: Duke University Press, 1939).

[2] In a book review, *American Sociological Review*, IV (December, 1939), 861.

those impassioned scholars who, in the depression of the 1930's, contended that in such times of crisis plodding research should be dropped and all effort applied to the urgent needs of the times. The crusty Sumner at Yale, who put the important words folkways and mores into the language and stated useful generalizations about the origins of customs and institutions, developed an interest somewhat the reverse of that of Ward and Ross and spent much of his teaching energy persuading students that it was dangerous to interfere with natural processes. Thus his sociology served as a pointer to the right in economic and political affairs, as Ward and Ross beckoned toward the left. Although this kind of activity filled his classes with attentive undergraduates, it did not build a living tradition. Sociology declined at Yale compared to its flourishing elsewhere and began to thrive again only after the importation of non-Yale men in the 1950's. Neither Sumner nor his disciple and successor Albert G. Keller seemed interested in building research methods. According to Small, "Professor Sumner rather early acquired the rank of a Yale tradition. Several of his students have told me that in their day he was lecturing on what might be described as *the sort of opinions that ought to be held on things in general by a Yale man*. They added that no one was supposed to have 'done' Yale as a gentleman should, without having taken at least one course with 'Billy' Sumner." [3]

Franklin H. Giddings organized a department of sociology at Columbia a year after the department at Chicago was established, and something of a potential contest for leadership was to be expected. Giddings, however, stumbled on the boulders of doctrine. The nineteenth-century prestige and promise of the evolutionary theory led him to tie sociology too closely to that course and to connect it in a somewhat doctrinaire spirit with economic determinism. His fondness for the explanatory power in his concept of like-mindedness also led him to ignore too many other promising directions of sociological inquiry.

The early Columbia approach may have suffered further from being too closely related to humanitarian interests and practical training in social work, a combination which has always appeared somewhat incompatible with scientific sociology. In announcing his plans for the

[3] Albion W. Small, "Fifty Years of Sociology in the United States—1865–1915," *American Journal of Sociology* (May, 1916), 184.

new department of sociology at Columbia in 1894, Giddings mentioned the "effective treatment of social problems" and the intention "to direct the students in practical sociological work" as among the major aims. General sociology was the foremost objective, but it was supposed to lead to "the more particular study" of such matters as "the growth and characteristics of the dependent, defective, and delinquent classes" and "pauperism, poor laws, methods of charity, crime, penology, and social ethics." [4]

Nevertheless, as stated in a previous chapter, Giddings made a major contribution through his advocacy and encouragement of the statistical method. This subject was already being taught at Columbia by Richmond Mayo-Smith before the organization of a sociology department, and Mayo-Smith's courses on Practical Statistics and the Science of Statistics were listed as part of the sociology offerings after 1893. The course on the Science of Statistics, which met two hours a week, seems primitive more than seventy years later, including as it did an examination of a great deal of published statistical material. At the end of a long description and almost as an afterthought, Giddings says: "Finally are considered the method of statistical observations, the value of the results obtained, the doctrine of free will, and the possibility of discovering social laws."

From these modest beginnings the development of statistics at Columbia flourished, and it was in this aspect of sociology that the university held the leadership at least until Ogburn went to Chicago. Eventually a series of sociologists came from the Columbia department who made further contributions by stimulating and developing statistical methods and by applying them in research. Besides Ogburn, mention should be made of F. Stuart Chapin, Frank A. Ross, Elbridge Sibley, Frank H. Hankins, Howard Woolston, James P. Lichtenberger, Howard W. Odum, Warren S. Thompson, John L. Gillin, and Malcolm M. Willey.

It is appropriate to speculate briefly on other differences in productivity between the successors of Small and those of his outstanding contemporaries in American sociology—Ward, Sumner, Cooley, Ross, and Giddings—whose works are more read today. Except for the soft-spoken Cooley, the others were more dominant personalities than

[4] Quoted from Howard W. Odum, *American Sociology* (New York: Longmans Green and Co., 1951, p. 61.

Small and they were outstanding in their vigor and self-confidence. It is probably significant that the first three presidents of the American Sociological Society were Ward, Sumner, and Giddings. Small was fourth, followed by the somewhat younger Ross. Cooley's gentler disposition may have been a reason for his later position, three terms after Ross.

Chicago's time lead may have been a minor factor in her growth, although it amounted to only a year ahead of Columbia. Nevertheless, in the younger city and the new university this department had a powerful commitment to build and a strong asset in the backing of the able and inventive William Rainey Harper. Able students came early and, as their numbers and influence grew, the word spread that a vigorous development of the new subject could be found at Chicago.

Probably the most important factor in the growth at Chicago was the intelligent perception by Small, accepted enthusiastically by his colleagues and successors, of the inhibiting consequences of doctrines, schools of thought, and authoritative leaders. Unlike Small's leading rivals who were confident that they had the right basic principles for a sociology and who sought to convert disciples in order to perpetuate through them competition with conflicting doctrines, the Chicago faculty renounced the principle of authority and encouraged open, modest searching in the spirit of an inductive science. Their students were taught to venture into the complex world of actuality, to bring in new information in quantities, and to devise and improve methods of extracting durable generalizations from it. If the new generalizations turned out to contradict the assertions of their teachers, they were encouraged to trust the evidence and follow the indicated trails.[5] If the results made obsolete some of the sociology being taught, it was regarded as a triumph for both student and teacher.

Some kind of connection prevails between the existence of schools

[5] In the brief concluding chapter of his *General Sociology* (Chicago: University of Chicago Press, 1905, pp. 728–729), Small wrote, "One cannot have made the foregoing argument in ignorance that to most minds it must seem a mere churning of words. . . . Men . . . honestly believe that sociology is profitless refinement of academic trifles. To this state of mind we must cheerfully respond: If sociology is profitless, by all means let it alone. . . . sociology, like all science and all philosophy, is a possible hindrance to action. On the other hand, action not sanctioned by science and philosophy is blind, and thought that stops short of the utmost comprehension of its object is impotent . . . To do the right thing, except by accident, in any social situation, we must rightly think the situation . . . Sociology aims to become the lens through which such insight may be possible."

of thought and the disposition to construct special terminology. While it is obvious that any science requires technical terms for distinctions and designations which are not readily made in ordinary discourse, the abandoned coinage of jargon appears to be a taste of the cultist. As consistent with their avoidance of a school discipline, the Chicago sociologists sought to transmit their knowledge in standard English and attempted to influence their graduate students to do likewise. When jargon appeared in the writings of enthusiastic cliques of young sociologists, it sometimes received open objections. No member of the Chicago department was more direct in calling attention to the absurd coinage of terms than was Faris, who on appropriate occasions used slashing book reviews to criticize the practice. The following examples may indicate something of the strength of his antijargon campaign.

" 'The authors of this book wrote with the purpose of originating in set events to the public who are supposed to terminate to them.' The meaning of the above statement may not be clear, but it is in the style and vocabulary the authors have chosen . . . The reviewer would feel justified in declining to comment on the book until it is rendered into good English . . . whatever the controlling motive may have been, it was neither modesty nor humility. Nor can the authors blame a reviewer if their book occasions an excitation of the hypothalamus with resulting emotions, not safely set down here. They have originated to me but I should like to originate to them in pair events and should fondly hope that they would terminate to me." [6]

"Numerous formulae and pseudo-equations are presented and impressively numbered, serving, in every instance, to repeat in symbols what has been said in plain English. In this way a mathematical appearance can be given to any statement. One could write, for example:

$$\text{Cl (Sym. Top)} < \text{Cl (GIM)}$$

in which Cl is clarity; Sym. indicates symbols; Top is topological; and GIM stands for good idiomatic English. On page 30, formula 9a appears thus:

$$\text{real}^{max} (\text{Ch}) < \text{real}^{max} (\text{Ad})$$

with the explanation that real means realism, max is maximum, Ch is Child, and Ad means Adult. It is then written out in words that the

[6] From *American Sociological Review*, VIII (April, 1943), 240–241.

maximum degree of realism which a child is able to show is less than that of the adult. In this way the discussion reaches 314 pages." [7]

The open exploratory spirit was characteristic of President Harper and Albion Small. Vigorous penetration into new fields to seek massive amounts of systematically gathered data was further encouraged by the example of W. I. Thomas, and soon after by Park and Burgess, and from then on by the rest of the second–generation faculty.

This deliberate and even determined avoidance of a constricting school of thought or doctrine allowed the students to profit from European sociological writings as well as from American sociologists, psychologists, anthropologists, and philosophers. While the social psychology developed by Dewey, Cooley, Mead, and others was found to be highly compatible with sociology as developed by Thomas, Park, and Burgess, the students were also encouraged and even required to read widely in other traditions. The result was a body of developing sociology incomparably broader in content than could be found in Ward, Sumner, or Giddings or in any one school of thought in Europe.

This openness to influences from other traditions was also reflected in the decision to bring Ogburn to Chicago from Columbia, thus enriching the local sociological content with the research-method emphasis that had been developing at Columbia. In that period no Chicago-trained sociologist was brought into the departments at Columbia or Yale. Brown first appointed a very young instructor from Chicago (the author) in 1931, but only after the last vestige of Ward's tradition had disappeared. Mid-century approached before Harvard ventured to bring in a representative of the Chicago sociology.

Another contrast between the Chicago faculty and Ward, Ross, and Sumner was in their regard for the application of knowledge to human welfare. The Chicago attitude was essentially that of pure science; that is, that while all knowledge is ultimately of potential value to human applications, it is worthwhile to pursue many intellectual questions without reference either to their immediate service or to the question of what particular applications the knowledge may have. In this view, the restriction of scholarly attention to the search for immediate alleviation of present problems may and generally does fail to solve such problems and also delays the development of the organized and tested knowledge which could be effective.

[7] From *American Sociological Review*, VII (February, 1942), 141.

Such an objective and scientific spirit was not the result of faculty inclinations. Burgess and Wirth in fact definitely leaned toward active concern with humanitarian matters, but for the most part they were intellectually convinced of the wisdom of building a science and tended to depart from this position only at times of special temptation in the later stages of their careers. Faris, who came from a theological and missionary career, acquired the scientific spirit from Dewey and other teachers in the course of his early study of psychology, and from the start he strongly urged his students to be objective. Park also had abundant human sympathies and political preferences, but he kept them under control in the same way. For example, in the subject of race relations, Park, a strong friend of the Negro peoples, successfully cultivated objective inquiry in this area by students of both white and Negro races.

While Ross at Wisconsin was still thundering about the yellow peril of Asia, Park was helping Negro students to investigate discrimination, prejudice, and even interracial violence with clinical objectivity. New students were sometimes astonished at the degree to which this was carried. For example, on January 14, 1921, Hayner entered in his diary that he listened to a report by Charles S. Johnson (later President of Fisk University) on research methods used in the study of the Chicago Race Riot of 1919 and noted that he "would not know he is a Negro from his cold-blooded presentation." Other students of race relations, including E. Franklin Frazier, were similarly successful in producing objective findings on a subject of popular passion, and the same detachment and objectivity were applied to a variety of subjects that involved public emotions.

Faris summed up this prevailing spirit at Chicago thus: "An objective science does not concern itself immediately with welfare. In order to be efficient it must be disinterested. But science, or knowledge, is always in the service of ends, and the ultimate justification of science, certainly the science of human nature, will be the service it can render to human welfare.

"The business of man is to seek good ends; intelligence is the instrument for making the quests effective; and science is the effort to perfect the instrument and to make it adequate." [8]

[8] Ellsworth Faris, *The Nature of Human Nature*, (New York: McGraw-Hill Book Co., 1937), p. 4.

Most of the graduate students in the 1920's embraced such a scientific temper; those who did not were likely to become impatient and transfer to another university or even to another field of study—some to welfare work or theology. The Chicago sociologist at work, however, was not lacking in human sympathies or concern for the good of humanity. He was confident that his way of working was the most valuable contribution he could make to mankind, and this conviction, shared with fellow workers in the discipline, stimulated his energetic quest for knowledge.

As an ever growing reward for adherence to the search for reliable knowledge, sociology gained acceptance, not only from other departments in the universities, but also very gradually from a wider public whose support is necessary for a subject to flourish. The eventual inclusion of the social sciences (including sociology but not social work) as one of the major divisions of the National Science Foundation could not have been achieved without understanding and support from the educated general public and the Congress of the United States. The scientific temper, which spread from Chicago and Columbia and later from many other departments of sociology, thus contributed importantly to the further financial support of objective research.

Throughout the 1920's at Chicago success built on success. The large student enrollment, the prominence of the faculty, the productivity of students and faculty and their pride in being independent of doctrine all combined to produce the high morale that characterized the department until well into the 1930's. These ideal conditions waned somewhat with the aging of the principal members of the second-generation faculty and were further disturbed by the pressures and distractions incident to the great depression and the Second World War. High competence and production has continued at Chicago, but leadership in sociology has become shared more widely with other universities as a more balanced' distribution of sociological effort prevails.[9]

If this descriptive characterization of an interesting period in the

---

[9] Research activity in the several social sciences at Chicago in the early and mid-1930's is described in a symposium edited by Leonard D. White, *Eleven Twenty-six: A Decade of Social Science Research* (Chicago: The University of Chicago Press, 1939).

history of sociology has any useful significance, it may be that both freedom and discipline favor creativity in the academic mind. The scholar thrives best when he preserves some independence from passions and doctrines, and when he uses effective self-control in employing the discipline of a scientific method.

APPENDIX A

Doctoral Dissertations in Sociology, University of Chicago, 1893-1935[1]

1895 Raymond, Jerome Hall *American Municipal Government*

Sanders, Frederic William *An Exposition in Outline of the Relation of Certain Economic Principles to Social Adjustment*

1896 Thomas, William Isaac *On a Difference of the Metabolism of the Sexes*

Vincent, George Edgar *Sociology and the Integration of Studies*

1897 Barrows, David Prescott *The Ethnobotany of Coahuila Indians of Southern California*

Clark, Hanna Belle (Mrs. Ambrose V. Powell) *The Public Schools of Chicago: A Sociological Study*

1897 Miller, Merton Leland *A Preliminary Study of the Pueblos of Taos, New Mexico*

1898 Howerth, Ira Woods *The Social Aim of Education*

1899 Ellwood, Charles Abram *Some Prolegomena of Social Psychology*

Gordon, William Clark *The Social Ideals of Alfred Tennyson as Related to His Time*

1900 Forrest, Jacob Dorsey *The Development of Industrial Organizations*

[1] The dissertation lists were furnished through the courtesy of Philip M. Hauser, Chairman of the Department of Sociology, University of Chicago, who began graduate study in 1929 and received the Ph.D. in 1938.

MacLean, Annie Marion   *The Acadian Element in the Population of Nova Scotia*

1901 Bushnell, Charles Joseph   *A Study of the Stock Yards Community at Chicago, as a Typical Example of the Bearing of Modern Industry upon Democracy, with Constructive Suggestions*

Gillette, John Morris   *The Culture Agencies of a Typical Manufacturing Group, South Chicago*

1902 Hayes, Edward Cary   *The Sociologist's Object of Attention*

1903 Hewes, Amy   *The Part of Invention in the Social Process*

1904 Adams, Romanzo Colfax   *A Technique for Sociological Research*

Riley, Thomas James   *A Study of the Higher Life of Chicago*

1905 Fleming, Herbert Easton   *Some Phases of the Production and Consumption of Literature in Chicago*

1906 Mumford, Eben   *The Beginning of Authority*

Rhoades, Mabel Carter   *A Case Study of Delinquent Boys in the Juvenile Court in Chicago*

Woods, Erville Bartlett   (*No title listed*)

1907 Dyer, Gustavus Walker   *Democracy in the South before the Civil War*

Woodhead, Howard   *The Social Significance of the Physical Development of Cities*

1908 North, Cecil Clare   *The Influence of Modern Social Relations upon Ethical Concepts*

1910 Bernard, Luther Lee   *The Transition to an Objective Standard of Control*

Fenton, Frances (Mrs. Edwin A. Park)   *The Influence of Newspaper Presentations upon the Growth of Crime and other Anti-Social Activity*

MacPherson, Hector   *Cooperative Credit Associations in the Province of Quebec*

1911 Bogardus, Emory Stephen   *The Relation of Fatigue to Industrial Accidents*

Reep, Samuel Nicholas   *Social Policy of Chicago Churches*

1912 House, Julius Temple   *Purpose, the Variant of Theory*

1913 Burgess, Ernest Watson   *The Function of Socialization in Social Evolution*

Steiner, Jesse Frederick   *The Japanese in America*

Sutherland, Edwin Hardin   *Unemployment and Public Employment Agencies*

1914 Elmer, Manuel Conrad   *Social Surveys of Urban Communities*

1915 Eubank, Earle Edward   *A Study of Family Desertion*

1917 Handman, Max   *The Beginnings of the Social Philosophy of Karl Marx*

1919 Blachley, Clarence Dan   *The Treatment of the Problem of Capital and Labor in Social Study Courses in the Churches*

Kawabe, Kisaburo   *The Japanese Newspaper and Its Relation to the Political Development of Modern Japan*

Queen, Stuart Alfred   *The Passing of the County Jail*

Reuter, Edward Byron   *The Mulatto in the United States: A Sociological and Psychological Study*

Stone, Raleigh Webster   *The Origin of the Survey Movement*

1920 Bodenhafer, Walter Blaine   *The Comparative Role of the Group Concept in Ward's Dynamic Sociology and Contemporary Sociology*

Carroll, Mollie Ray   *The Attitude of the American Federation of Labor toward Legislation and Politics*

Horak, Jacob   *The Assimilation of the Czechs in Chicago*

Jensen, Howard Eikenberry   *The Rise of Religious Journalism in the United States*

Smith, William Carlson   *Conflict and Fusion of Cultures as Typified by the Ao Nagas of India*

1921 McKenzie, Roderick Duncan   *The Neighborhood: A Study of Local Life in Columbus, Ohio*

Rainwater, Clarence Elmer   *The Evolution of the Play Movement in the United States: Its Structure and Function*

Ratcliffe, Samuel Caleb   *Pauper Law and Institutions in Illinois*

Sanderson, Dwight   *The Rural Community: A Social Unit*

1922 Bickham, Martin Hays   *The Scientific Antecedents of the Sociology of Auguste Comte*

Detweiler, Frederick German   *The Negro Press in the United States*

Rossouw, George S. H.   *Nationalism and Language*

1923 Hayner, Norman Sylvester *The Sociology of Hotel Life*

1924 Barnhart, Kenneth Edwin *The Evolution of Social Consciousness in Methodism*

Hiller, Ernest Theodore *The Strike as Group Behavior: A Study in the Process and Technique of Control of the Striking Group*

House, Floyd Nelson *Industrial Morale: An Essay in the Sociology of Industrial Control*

Mowrer, Ernest Russell *Family Disorganization—An Introduction to a Sociological Analysis*

Price, Maurice Thomas *Protestant Missions as Culture Contact*

Young, Erle Fiske *Race Prejudice*

1925 Daniel, William Andrew *Negro Theological Seminary Survey*

Karpf, Fay Berger *American Social Psychology and Its European Background*

Krueger, Ernst Theodor *Autobiographical Documents and Personality*

Reckless, Walter Cade *The Natural History of Vice Areas in Chicago*

Roest, Pieter Kornelis *"Krotona," Ojai, California and "Olcott," Wheaton, Illinois*

Wang, Tsi Chang *The Youth Movement in China*

1926 DeGraff, Harmon Opdike *A Study of the Juvenile Court of Iowa with Special Reference to Des Moines*

Janzen, Cornelius Cicero *A Social Study of the Mennonite Settlement in the Counties of Marion, McPherson, Harvey, Reno, and Butler, Kansas*

Shonle, Ruth (Mrs. Jordon T. Cavan) *Suicide—A Study of Personal Disorganization*

Simpson, Eyler Newton *Wishes: A Study in Social Psychology*

Thrasher, Frederic Milton *The Gang: A Study of 1,313 Gangs in Chicago*

Wirth, Louis *The Ghetto: A Study in Isolation*

1927 Shideler, Ernest Hugh *The Chain Store: A Study of the Ecological Organization of a Modern City*

White, Leslie A. *Medicine Societies of the Southwest*

1928 Blumer, Herbert *Method in Social Psychology*

Gower, Charlotte Day *The Supernatural Patron in Sicilian Life*

Hughes, Everett Cherrington   *A Study of a Secular Institution: The Chicago Real Estate Board*

Kawamura, Tadao   *The Class Conflict in Japan as Affected by the Expansion of Japanese Industry and Trade*

McCluer, Franc Lewis   *Living Conditions among Wage-Earning Families in Forty-One Blocks in Chicago* (1923)

Mueller, John Henry   (*No title listed*)

Redfield, Robert   *A Plan for the Study of Tepoztlan, Mexico*

Wu, Ching Chao   *The Chinese in the United States*

1929 Kincheloe, Samuel Clarence   *The Prophet: A Study of the Sociology of Leadership*

Kuhlman, Augustus Frederick   *Crime and Punishment in Missouri: A Study of the Social Forces in the Trial and Error Process of Penal Reform*

McCormick, Thomas Carson   *Rural Unrest: A Sociological Investigation of Rural Movements in the United States*

Neumeyer, Martin Henry   *Conscience: A Socio-Psychological Study*

1930 Becker, Howard Paul   *Ionia and Athens: Studies in Secularization*

Brown, William Oscar   *Race Prejudice: A Sociological Study*

Cressey, Paul Frederick   *The Succession of Cultural Groups in the City of Chicago*

Rosenquist, Carl M.   *A Sociological Study of the Swedes of Texas*

Stonequist, Everett Verner   *The Marginal Man: A Study in the Subjective Aspects of Cultural Conflict*

Stouffer, Samuel Andrew   *An Experimental Comparison of Statistical and Case History Methods of Attitude Research*

Watson, Walter Thompson   *Division of Labor: A Study in the Sociology and Social Psychology of Work Satisfaction*

Winston, Ellen Black   *A Statistical Study of Mental Disease*

1931 Clark, Carroll DeWitt   *News: A Sociological Study*

Dollard, John   *The Changing Functions of the American Family*

Faris, Robert E. Lee   *An Ecological Study of Insanity in the City*

Frazier, Edward Franklin   *The Negro Family in Chicago*

Koshuk, Ruth Pearson   *A Comparative Study of Social Contacts Involving Play Material in Four Pre-School Groups*

Lind, Andrew William   *Economic Succession and Racial Invasion in Hawaii*

Quinn, James Alfred   *Sublimation—A Study of a Social Process*

1932 Palmer, Vivien Marie   *The Primary Settlement Area as a Unit of Urban Growth and Organization*

Strow, Carl William   *The Human Resources of a Community*

Thompson, Edgar Tristram   *The Plantation*

Webster, Edward Jerome   *Reform: A Sociological Study*

1933 Blumenthal, Albert Bailie   *A Sociological Study of a Small Town*

Cottrell, Leonard Slater, Jr.   *The Reliability and Validity of a Marriage Study Schedule*

1934 Doyle, Bertram   *The Etiquette of Race Relations in the South*

Montgomery, Edward Wilkerson   *The Urbanization of Rural Recreation*

Yen, Ching Yeh   *Crime in Relation to Social Change in China*

1935 Roper, Marion Wesley   *The City and the Primary Group*

Van Vechten, Courtlandt Churchill   *A Study of Success and Failure of One Thousand Delinquents Committed to a Boys' Republic*

Master's Dissertations in Sociology, University of Chicago, 1893-1935

1893 Barnes, Clifford Webster *Stages in the Theological Development of Martin Luther*

1894 Atkinson, David Clarence *Attempt of Chicago to Meet the Positive Needs of the Community*

Howert, Ira Woods *Are the Italians a Dangerous Class?*

Learned, Henry Barrett *The Social Philosophy of Adam Smith*

1897 MacLean, Annie Marion *Factory Legislation for Women in the United States*

1898 Goodrich, Henrietta Isman (Mrs. B. J. Rothwell) *Laboratory Methods in House Sanitation, Together with an Outline of Class-Room Instruction*

1899 Harmon, Alta Annette *University Extension for Rural Communities*

1900 Auten, Nellie Mason *Some Phases of the Sweating System in Chicago*

1902 Frink, Fred Goodrich *The Garbage Problem in Chicago*

Klink, Jane Seymour *The Relation of the Medicine Man to the Educational System of the Early Ages of North America*

Thompson, Carl Dean *The Need of Cooperation of the Rochdale Type*

Thompson, Edwin Elbert *The Social Development of Indianapolis*

1903 Work, Monroe Nathan *The Negro Real-Estate Owner in Chicago*

1904 Benedict, Laura Estelle Watson   *The Hunting Pattern of Mind as Expressed in Totemism among the North American Indians*

Randall, James Garfield   *The Sunday Kindergarten*

1905 McLearie, John   *The Modern Treatment of the American Negro*

Newlin, Thomas   (*No thesis required*)

Zook, Ephraim Jacob   *Social Tendencies among the American Mennonites*

1906 Elam, Harvey William   *Outlines of Rural Community Life*

Henninger, John Wesley   (*No thesis required*)

Magee, James Dysart   (*No thesis required*)

Stephens, George Asbury   *The Juvenile Court System of Kansas*

1907 Dean, John Alvin   *Mackaye's Economy of Happiness*

Lermit, Geraldine   (*No thesis required*)

Scheftel, Yetta   *Persistence of Poverty*

1908 Anderson, Olive Orton (Mrs. Elwood O.)   *The Chicago Teachers' Federation*

Lamb, Ruby Lee (Mrs. John M. Miner)   *The First Three Years of Paul's Career as a Christian*

MacPherson, Hector   (*No thesis required*)

Waites, Bennett Taylor   *Child-Labor in the Cotton Mills of Alabama*

Woo, Tsing Nyuh   (*No thesis required*)

Woods, Lebbeus   *The Methodology of Carl Menger*

1909 Brandenburg, Samuel Jacob   (*No thesis required*)

1910 McCord, Robert Bryan   *The Morality of the American Negro*

Peterson, Otto Edward   *A Comparative Study of Mill's Utilitarianism and Small's Functional System of Ethics*

Tinney, Mary Catherine   *Catholic Charities with Illustrations from Chicago*

1911 Hammond, Juliet   *A Problem in the Psychology of Social Work*

Mangold, William Christopher   *The Boycott as a Means of Social Control*

Matzinger, Philip Frederick   *A Study of the Effect of Primitive Art upon Primitive Morals*

1912 Baker, Elizabeth Whitemore   *The Social and Economic Condition of Women Teachers in the United States*

Beneke, Herman Henry   *A Comparison of White Boys and Adult Indian Groups*

Bizzell, William Bennett   *Variability and Socialization*

Bruder, Victor William   *The Relation of Religion to the "On-Going" of the Social Process*

Erickson, J. Edward   *A Neglected Element in Representative Government*

Hursh, Edwin May   *The Training of the Child among Primitive African Peoples*

Martin, Vella Vernelle   *A Study of Family Schedules*

Newberry, Ruth (Mrs. William A. Thomas)   *Origin and Criticism of Funds to Parents' Act*

Perigord, Paul Helie   *Catholic Social Action in France*

Smith, Walter Marion   *The Relation of Education to Social Progress*

1913 Butler, Walter Hudson   *The Family as an Organ of Control*

Gilkeson, Rebecca Baxter   *Economic and Social Survey of Augusta County, Virginia, 1880–1910*

Kolb, John Harrison   *Arbitration in the Chicago Street-car Controversy of 1912*

McElroy, Georgia Pearl (Mrs. Arthur C. Hunt)   *(No thesis required)*

Queen, Stuart Alfred   *The Beginnings of Public Relief*

Souers, Ralph Edward   *Industrial Workers of the World*

1914 Coleman, Paul Evans   *The Necessity of Compulsory Sickness Insurance*

Holst, Bertram Paul   *The History and Present Status of Eugenics as a Theory*

Sager, Gertrude Aileen   *The Italian Women and Girls of Chicago*

Zee, Treusinn Zoen   *(No thesis required)*

1915 Blount, Elmina Louise   *Suggestion and Imitation: Forms of Social Interaction*

Hoover, Joe Wenger   *Social Attitude among the Mennonites*

Zeeb, Frieda Bertha   *The Mobility of the German Women*

1916 Mann, Albert Russell   *Some Effects of the Social Concept on Recent Economic Theory*

Morrow, Verle   *The Negro Familial Sentiments*

Saito, Waichi   *The Systems of Sociology*

Sletten, Joseph Nathaniel   *Martin Luther's Attitudes and Values*

1917 Church, Clarence Cecil   *Types of Social Groups*

Forrest, Elizabeth   *Municipal Reference Libraries in Relation to Social Control*

McClintock, Euphemia E.   (*No thesis required*)

Shideler, Ernest Hugh   *A Comparative Study of Parental Conditions of Juvenile Delinquents in the United States*

1918 Marrs, James Wyatt   *Attitude of Typical Individuals toward Birth Control*

Pitlik, Samuel   *The Messianic Myths: Its Role in the Life of the Jewish People*

Takanashi Taka   *The Status of Women under Modern Conditions of Japanese Life*

Thrasher, Frederic Milton   *The Boy Scout Movement as a Socializing Agency*

Young, Kimball   *Sociological Study of a Disintegrated Neighborhood*

1919 Bickham, Martin Hayes   *The Relations of Sociology and Religion from 1865 to 1915*

Green, Loraine Richardson   *The Rise of Race Consciousness in the American Negro*

Niemi, Clemens   *Americanization of the Finnish People in Houghton County, Michigan*

Rossouw, George S. H.   *The Family and Social Life of the Dutch-Speaking South African: A Study of Familism as a Factor in Social Organization*

1920 Davis, Thomas Russell   *Negro Servitude in the United States*

Krueger, Ernest Theodor   *Life History Case Studies in Temperaments and Social Attitudes of College Freshmen*

Young, Erle Fisk   *Suggestions for the Formulation of a Program of Moral Training in the United States Army: A Preliminary Examination*

1921 Hayner, Norman Sylvester   *The Effects of Prohibition on Packingtown*

Kuhlman, Augustus Frederick   *The Social Survey of the City of Jackson and Madison County, Tennessee*

Meloy, Olga May (Mrs. A. L. Carter) *The Harrisburg Playground System*

Mowrer, Ernest Russell *A Study of the Variance between the Legal Grounds for Divorce and the Natural Causes of Family Disintegration as Indicated by Court Records*

Sato, Kenoske *Sociological Thought in the Philosophy of John Dewey*

Stone, William Bradley *Measuring the Ability of Seventh, Eighth, and Ninth Grade Pupils to Read a Narrative*

Yokoyama, Hidesaburo *Japanese Associations in America*

1922 Buchan, Evelyn (Mrs. E. B. Crook) *The Delinquency of Girls*

Fu, Daniel Chich *Ancestor Worship as a Type of Social Control*

Johnson, Guy B. *The New Ku Klux Movement*

Lewis, Sarah Florence (Pen name Sonnia Lee) *Social Aspects of Post-War Immigrant Jews*

Meroney, William Penn *The Town Church and the Modern Home*

Neely, Anne Elizabeth *The Foreign Student on the American Campus*

Rogers, Beryl (Mrs. McClasky) *A Modern Mining Community: A Sociological Study*

Rosenthal, Harriet Catherine (Mrs. Ernest R. Mowrer) *The Intermarriage of Jew and Gentile: A Study in Cultural Conflicts and Accommodation*

Sell, Harry Bird *The American Federation of Labor and The Labor Party Idea*

Sie, Hsuincher H. *The Chinese Student Movement in 1919–1920*

1923 Burton, Ernest Richmond *Employees' Representation*

Daniel, William Andrew *Bi-Racial Organization*

Kato, Masuo *The Mechanism of Expressive Behavior in the Growth of Self*

Moore, Henry Lewis Davis *A Study of the Vocational Choices and Motives of a Selected Group of Grammar School Children*

Shonle, Ruth (Mrs. Cavan) *The Isolated Religious Sect*

1924 Doyle, Bertram Wilbur *Racial Traits of the Negro as Negroes Assign Them to Themselves*

Frank, Jacob Louis *The Germanic or Nordic Race Theory*

Halley, Lois Kate *A Study of Motion Pictures in Chicago as a Medium of Communication*

Krout, Maurice Haim *Theories and Methods in American Sociology 1872–1922*

Simpson, Eyler Newton *The Use of Literary Materials in the Study of Wishes and Personality Types*

Vold, George Bryan *Evidences of the Influence of Herbert Spencer upon the Sociological Writings of Franklin H. Giddings*

1925 Anderson, Nels *The Hobo*

Boorman, William Ryland *A Suggested Technique for Vocational Guidance Analysis*

Davis, Ada Jeanette *A Social Psychological Study of Musicians*

Nyi, Vong-Kyih *The Change in the Status of Chinese Women*

Tan, Shao Hwa *Chinese Characters: Their Nature, Origin and Development*

Waller, Willard Walter *Fluctuations in the Severity of the Punishment of Criminals from the XI to the XX centuries*

Wirth, Louis *Culture Conflicts in the Immigrant Family*

1926 Butcher, William Arthur *Juvenile Delinquency in a Rapidly Growing City*

Carter, William Paul *A Social Psychological Study of the Only Child in the Family*

Conway, Paul Raymond *The Apartment House Dweller: A Study of the Social Change in the Hyde Park Community*

Emery, Julia *The Modern Symphony Orchestra: A Study in Social Control*

Gower, Charlotte Day *Origin and Spread of Antillean Culture*

Hajicek, Stanley Thomas *Case Study of Restlessness*

Jenkins, Francis Raymond *The Evolution of Negro Race-Consciousness*

Stephan, Frederick Franklin *Some Social Aspects of the Telephone*

Wu, Ching Chao *Chinese Immigration in the Pacific Area*

1927 Bartlett, Harriet Moulton *The Injured Workman*

Chaffee, Grace Earhart *A Sociological Investigation of the Amana and Amish-Mennonite Communities*

Crooks, Elza Allen *Social Development of the Nineteenth Century and Theological Activity*

Giffen, Naomi Musmaker *Differences in the Lives of Men and Women Eskimo in Society, with Special Reference to the Economic Life*

Krogman, Wilton Marion *Problems and Methods in the Study of the Culture Represented in the Ohio Mounds*

MacGill, Helen Elizabeth Gregory (Mrs. Everett C. Hughes) *Land Values: An Ecological Factor in the Community of South Chicago*

1928 Bittner, Walton Simon *Attitude and Opinions on Immigration and Birth Control*

Black, Ellen Engelmann (Mrs. Sanford Winston) *A Study of the Diffusion of Culture in a Relatively Isolated Mountain County*

David, George Franklin *Personnel Studies of College Girls*

Glick, Clarence Elmer *Winnetka: A Study of a Residential Suburban Community*

Leiffer, Murray Howard *The Boys' Court of Chicago*

McAfee, Mildred Helen *The Y.W.C.A.: A Case Study of a Religious Movement*

Montgomery, Edward Wilkerson *The Social Attitudes of the American Negro on the Race Problem*

Nesbitt, Paul Homer *A Study of the Aurignacian Site, La Ruth (France)*

Pond, Alonzo William *A Contribution to the Study of Prehistoric Man in Algeria, North Africa*

Wiley, James Hundley *A Study of Chinese Prostitution*

1929 Cressey, Paul Goalby *The Closed Dance Hall in Chicago*

Duflot, Joseph Leo *A Social Psychological Study of the Failing Student in High School and College*

Mangus, Arthur Raymond *The Church and Politics: A Study of the Work of the Commission on Political Action of the Chicago Church Federation*

Nelson, Raymond Edward *A Study of an Isolated Industrial Community*

Newcomb, Ruth Gustafson *An Analysis of the Concept Personality Type*

Pedersen, Laura Mayne *Some Sociological Aspects of Educational Reforms*

Scott, Chester Curtis *A Study of the Boys' Work Program of a Social Settlement in Its Relation to Delinquency*

Shapiro, Dena Evelyn *Indian Tribes and Trails of the Chicago Region: A Preliminary Study of the Influence of the Indian on the Early White Settler*

Sweeney, Harold Walter *Certain Aspects of Inventions in Their Relation to Cultural Evolution*

1930 Baker, Paul *Opinions on Punishment: Their Content and Rationale*

Barton, Olive Lillian *Social Psychology in the Interpreting and Furthering of Personality Adjustments*

Dollard, John *The Pre-Machine American Family*

Elowson, Margueritte Luesing *Some Aspects of the Cook County Juvenile Court in Relation to the Readjustment of the Delinquent Girl*

Faris, Robert E. Lee *The Development of the Philosophy Underlying the Durkheim School of Social Theory*

Newcomb, Charles Shelton *A Single Numerical Index of Age and Sex Distribution of Population*

Peirce, Adah Marie *An Analysis of the Changes in the Concepts of Three Hundred Forty-Six Freshmen Students at Stephens College*

Price, Mildred (Mrs. Harold R. Coy) *The Effects of an Adult Education Project upon a Group of Industrial Women*

Riegel, Ernest Franklin *A Study of a Social Settlement in an Industrial Community with Special Reference to Juvenile Delinquency*

Stephan, Anthony Steven *Factors Making For and Retarding Success in Sample Chicago Public-School Community Centers*

Woolbert, Helen Griffin *Type of Social Philosophy as a Function of Father-Son Relationship*

Woolbert, Richard Latham *The Social Effect of the Radio*

1931 Abassi, Mostafa *The Rise of Nationalism in Persia*

Carmichael, Mack Philip *The Negro Family in Texas*

Eisendrath, Ruth Minna *The Effect of the Urban Environment upon a Large Family Group*

Elliott, Melissa Mae *Negro News and News Agencies*

Guignard, Clara (Mrs. Robert E. L. Faris) *The Vocational Guidance Movement*

Hall, Martha Haygood *The Nursemaid: A Social Psychological Study of an Occupational Group*

Hurd, Frederick   *A Study in the Securing of Life History Documents and Their Statistical Analysis*

Rosario, Jose Colomban   *Historical Development of the Jibaro of Puerto Rico and His Present-day Attitudes toward Society*

Russell, Daniel   *The Roadhouse: A Study of Commercialized Amusements in the Environs of Chicago*

Stuart, Johannes   *Study of Divorce in Cook County*

Talbot, Nell Snow   *Some Factors in the 1928 Presidential Elections*

1932 Austin, Anne L.   *The Sociology of Professionalization as Shown by Nursing*

Beck, Dorothy Fahs (Mrs. H. P. Beck)   *The Development of the Dental Profession in the United States: A Study in the Natural History of a Profession*

Beckmire, Regena Marie   *The Study of Highland Park as a Residential Suburb*

Dai, Bingham   *Speaking with Tongues or Glossolalia*

Goldeen, Freda (Mrs. Rasael Silver)   *The Concept "Society" in Sociology*

Hill, Betty M.   *A Comparative Study of Delinquency in Four National Groups in Cook County Juvenile Court in 1930*

Johnson, Earl Shepard   *The Ecology of the Physician*

Lang, Richard Otto   *Variance, by Occupation, of Happiness or Unhappiness in Marriage Rated by Acquaintances of the Married Couples*

Moses, Earl Richard   *Community Factors in Negro Delinquency*

Pitts, George Bristol Jr.   *A Study in the Determination of Vocational Interest*

1933 Alexander, Chester S.   *The Young Man Employed in the Loop*

Hauser, Philip M.   *Motion Pictures in Penal and Correctional Institutions: A Study of the Reactions of Prisoners to Movies*

Hill, Estelle Chetola (Mrs. A. H. Scott)   *The Economic Factor in the Roosevelt-Hoover Election*

Pierson, R. Donald   *A Study in Fashion as Indicated by Facial Adornment*

Reed, John Paul   *Some Basic Factors in the Development of Public Opinion in Japan*

Su, Karl Yu   *An Analysis of Child Personality by Means of the Neurotic Inventory*

1934 Barlow, Carrie M.   *Auburn Gresham: The Survey of a Local Community*

Chen, Ifu   *The Old Chinese Family: The Study of Familial Control*

Diehl, Lois   *The Young Women's Christian Association in Estonia. A Study in the Transplanting of an Institution*

LaViolette, Forrest E.   *Some Problems Relating to the Concept of Culture*

Maurer, Pearl C. (Mrs.)   *A Study of Personality Adjustment of 600 Children in the Sixth, Seventh and Eighth Grades*

Merrill, Francis Ellsworth   *The News and the Money Market*

Noss, Theodore K.   *The Awakening of the Quaker Movement against Negro Slavery in Colonial Pennsylvania and West New Jersey*

Plumley, Margaret Lovell   *Comparative Study of Self and Friends' Ratings of Seventy-one Personality Traits*

Severson, Alfred L.   *Discrimination Against the Jews in Employment in Chicago Offices, with Particular Reference to Four Groups of Offices*

1935 Handsaker, Lois M.   *Motivation of Professional Choice among Social Workers*

Niles, Katherine E.   *A Study in the Sociology of Reading*

Pfeil, Walter   *Workers' Education in Chicago*

Weinberg, S. Kirson   *A Study of Isolation among Chicago Shelterhouse Men*

INDEX OF NAMES

INDEX OF SUBJECTS